Rapid Fire Opening

Introduction

Time is of the essence when opening a bar. Electric and rent bills pile up, companies want payment for equipment, suppliers want money for inventory, and no one gives a damn whether or not you are bringing in any cash yet. Until you are open and slinging drinks across the bar, you'll have to pay for every single expense out of pocket. That's why the faster you can get your bar up and running, the better chance you have of succeeding in the long run.

I once opened a bar in 28 days after obtaining a lease. Now, I don't expect everyone who reads this to be able to set up a bar in that amount of time. I've had years of practice, while I'm assuming you haven't. What I can assure you is that if you study my program and follow my steps closely, you will save yourself countless hours and thousands of dollars. Maybe one day you will even beat my opening record and you better contact me and tell me how you did it.

I wasn't always successful at getting bars open fast and believe me I made mistakes that cost me tens of thousands of dollars before I even opened the doors to the public. I once even had to walk away from one lease contract because I didn't do the proper homework before I started. I created this program to share my knowledge, so good people like YOU won't have to go through the same headaches I've experienced.

Besides getting bars up and running fast, I attribute my success in the bar business to 3 other key factors:

1) Exploiting profitable market niches.

2) Choosing great locations.

3) Keeping my start-up expenses low, to maximize future profits.

I cover all of these factors throughout the manual, so you can learn to open successful bars the same exact way I do.

How To Use This book

My bar opening program consists of 25 easy to follow steps, grouped into 5 phases. Some phases require you to complete the steps simultaneously (even though they are numbered for organizational purposes), while other phases require you to complete the steps in order. I will tell you at the beginning of each phase how to proceed.

I recommend reading through the manual from start to finish a few times before you get started with your own bar. That way when the time comes to start your bar, the steps will be engrained and everything will flow easier. Please don't forget to review the DVD portion of the program as well.

When you come across this icon of the man with the torch, pay attention! I use this guy when I'm about to give some important pro advice and pass you the "Torch of Knowledge" (silly I know, but you get my point).

When you go through the program, please realize that it's important for you to learn every single operation of your bar without exception. If you decide to hire a manager, then they too must learn everything (and I do mean everything). From plunging clogged toilets to working/maintaining all equipment, both of you must know the ropes so you can teach staff members and also step in as substitutes, should someone quit mid-shift. I once had a cook quit mid-shift and it took me a week to find another replacement. If I stopped serving food for that week, our reputation and business would have suffered big time. That's why I stepped in and worked all week on the cook line pumping out food so business stayed thriving. It wasn't exactly the most enjoyable option, but definitely the smartest.

I know I can prepare you well for your journey, but how you handle the fine details is up to you. Keep a positive attitude and a bottle of Jim Beam close and you can get through anything. I'm just joking about the Jim Beam though. Jim is not the answer. Now let's begin your new journey….

Phase 1: Pre-Bar

Attack Steps in Order

Step 1: Gut Check

The bar business is unlike any other…are you truly ready for what's in store? Before you go any further answer the following questions to get an idea of how ready you truly are.

Question 1:
Are you prepared to work long hours, holidays, and/or weekends?

Question 2:
If you have a family, are they supportive and prepared for what's to come?

Question 3:
Would you consider yourself personable? For example, do you enjoy being around large groups of people and interacting with them?

Question 4:
Do you consider yourself a leader or a follower?

Question 5:
Have you written a business plan yet?

Question 6:
Do you have enough startup capital? If not, how are you going to find funds?

Question 7:
Where are you financially (savings vs. debt)?

Question 8:
Do you enjoy challenges and handle adversity well?

Question 9:
Are you trying to set up a revenue stream or just looking to own a bar where you drink and party for free?

Question 10:
Are you prepared to be an active manager of your business or do you plan on giving all responsibility to someone else?

Question 11:
If you have a day job, are you willing to quit?

Question 12:
What are your financial goals?

Okay, let's discuss your answers…..

Question 1:
To be successful in this business you must be prepared to work long hours even on weekends and holidays. 16-18 hour days are not unusual especially when you are in the early stages of construction and opening. Even when your business gets going most bars are open for lunch and stay open into the early am hours. If you are going to be an active manager, your job goes past business hours to ensure everything is done properly.

When you finally have a successful system in place and find some employees you can count on, your life should get easier. However, problems always find a way to come up and you never know when you might have to rush to the bar at 3 or 4 in the morning.

Question 2:
Your family needs to know beforehand that owning a bar is very time consuming. If they understand this in the beginning I guarantee you will have less headaches down the road. A supportive family will definitely help in your success.

Question 3:
This line of work is not for you if you enjoy keeping to yourself. You need to mingle with customers, network in the community, and effectively manage staff. If you get frustrated easily with personalities different than yours then stop reading this now and consider a new line of work!

On the other hand, if you consider yourself personable and don't mind networking and mingling, then get ready for some fun. You are going to meet a lot of new and different people and build profitable relationships that could potentially make your bar the best around.

Question 4:
Since you are getting ready to start your own business you need to do a serious gut check on this one. Only leaders succeed in this business. You are going to have many people influencing you to do things differently and go against what you know is right. You must be able to take initiative and get things done without having others around to motivate you.

You must have the character to act firmly and with confidence. You will have to deal with employees who alter their uniforms or come in 30 minutes late for their shift. On the other side, you have to manage customers as well. Some customers will try and influence you to take 5 rounds of shots and then get you to come with them to the bar next door. You must be able to stay on track and commit yourself to your business at all times.   If you don't have much discipline in your regular job then you probably going to have a hard time succeeding among all the negative temptation in the bar business.

Question 5:
Writing up a business plan is absolutely necessary in the initial stages of planning. You need a business plan to create a blue print for future success, so definitely spend the time typing this up and making it look more professional by adding a presentation cover.

If you are looking for investors, business partners, or any other institutional backing for your bar then you must have a business plan ready to show. Even when you find the right real estate for your bar it's not a bad idea to have a copy to present to landlords, because it demonstrates professionalism and hopefully encourages them to do business with you (more on business plans in Step 6).

Question 6:
If you think you have enough startup capital think again. There are many expenses that come as surprises and if you aren't over prepared you risk the chance of holding up your opening and incurring even more expenses. I find it's good practice to budget for 20-30% more than you think you might need.

Also, if you have investing partners and/or other funding lined up make sure that cash is in the business account and ready to go before you sign the lease or spend money on any expenses. Never spend cash that isn't already in your possession (more on finding financing in Step 7).

Question 7:
I wouldn't suggest getting into this business without $10k saved away. Even if you have investors and/or other financing for everything you won't be bringing money in the door for a month or two and living off credit cards isn't smart. If you don't have any savings, make it a goal to put money into savings every week. Even putting $50 a week into savings is a huge start in the right direction.

Also, you need to analyze your current debt situation. I suggest you look up your credit score to know exactly where you are. A bad credit score will hurt your chances of obtaining loans as well as getting approved for property leases and/or equipment.   If you don't have a good credit score, set goals to chip away at your bad debt (i.e. credit card bills and/or delinquent bills). It took me years after college to get rid of all my credit card debt (including my bad spending habits), but without taking care of my debt, I would never have been so successful in my career.

Question 8:
Owning a business is extremely stressful at times. You can't just fake a sick day like you could if you were an employee and if you don't hit your numbers for the month no one but you is directly affected or really cares. This business can make you rich or it can take away your savings and security if you don't do things right. The reality is that 9 out of every 10 start-ups fail, so with these odds you better find joy in the day-to-day challenges and the motivation to work hard and get things done.

Question 9:
Okay, so you probably thought I was joking with this question, but quite the contrary. First off, no drink at your bar is ever going to be free for you. You will always be paying for it somehow.

Secondly, I know too many owners who have squandered their success away from partying too hard and too often at their place of work. This will be your job and like any other job, professional behavior goes a long way towards success. If you are serious about the longevity and profitability of your business be extremely careful about the image you portray at your bar.

Question 10:
Either way you answered this question you pass, however, the important part is that you know the positives and negatives of each choice. Hiring a manager to control the operation of your bar is fine, but that doesn't mean you shouldn't be going over the numbers on a daily basis.

No one is going to look after your investment like you will, so always remember that and act accordingly. Many employees in the bar business make a career out of stealing from owners.

Question 11:
Opening a bar without quitting your day job is next to impossible. If you have the money to hire someone to do everything for you, then you don't count because you are the minority! Unless you hire an expert opening manager you are better off quitting your day job and managing the opening on your own, that is, if you are truly serious about succeeding in this business and have enough money saved away to last you a few months.

Question 12:
Does part of your answer have something to do with making a lot of money? Just remember starting your own bar is not a get rich quick scheme by any means. You can make great money and set yourself up for a nice stream of revenue, however, make sure you set realistic goals especially for your first year when your focus is on growing your business.

Now that you are in the right frame of mind to succeed in this business let's move on to the next step…..

ONLINE RESOURCES:

1) Find your credit score:
http://www.annualcreditreport.com
This site allows you to obtain your credit score for free once every 12 months.

http://www.freecreditreport.com
This site let's you have your first credit report free, but if you don't cancel your membership within the "trial" period you incur a monthly fee. If your score needs improvement then the monthly service may be worth the money so you can monitor any changes more frequently.

Step 2: Choose a Theme

When choosing a theme I first want you to narrow down a 10-mile area that you would like to open a bar in. If you have always wanted to start an upscale wine bar, but there are already 2 successful wine bars within 10 miles then I would consider starting a different type of bar. If you are dead set on sticking with a certain bar concept then stay flexible with the location and find an area that really needs your concept.

There many types of bar themes to choose. A few to consider include:
- Sports
- Wine
- Martini
- Tavern/Saloon/Pub
- Nationality Specific (ex: Irish Pub, German, English Pub)
- Lounge
- Country
- Special Group (ex: Gay/Lesbian, Biker)
- Karaoke
- Beach
- Piano
- Tapas
- Neighborhood
- College

If none of these bar themes interest you then by all means create something new. Find a theme that hasn't been done before. A friend recently told me about a popular bar in Nashville, TN that's designed to look like a trailer park with artificial turf on the floor and plastic lawn furniture everywhere….now talk about creative. I just can't wait for my next trip to Nashville to see that bar.

The main goal in choosing a bar theme is first figuring out what market niche hasn't been filled by the other bars in the area. Many bar owners fail because they choose a theme they want and not a theme that the area really needs. I suggest you stay flexible in your theme choice and complete *Steps 2 and 3* before you make your final decision.

Personally, I only open bars that cater to market niches that haven't been exploited. I never get my heart set on a concept if it's not appropriate in the area I'm looking to build. For example, I opened a German bar and restaurant in an area where no bar was targeting the largest population segment of upper middle class 40-60 year olds. German bars typically attract more of a middle age crowd, so through my research I felt that a German bar would satisfy the area's need. Another supporting argument for my German theme was the fact that the closest

German bar or restaurant was well over 25 miles away, so I knew that I had found a unique theme for the area that had the potential to become very success.

If you need some help choosing a bar theme start with the questions in Section 1 to help you brainstorm. If you already have an idea for your bar proceed to the questions in Section 2.

Section 1: Choosing a Bar Theme

1) What type of bars do you enjoy going to?

2) What bars have you visited that really stand out in your mind? What makes them different?

3) What are some of the most popular bars in your area?

4) What bars have not succeeded in the area? What was their downfall?

5) What sort of bar would you like to see open in your area that does not exist right now?

Section 2: Now that you have a theme in mind use these questions to challenge your idea

1) What group of people do you plan to target? (i.e. white or blue collar people, specific age group, etc.)

2) How many bars in the area do you feel would be in direct competition for your bar? (Direct competition is a bar with a similar theme within 10 miles)

3) How will your bar differ from your competition to develop a strong customer base?

4) If your theme does not exist in the area, why do you think your idea would be successful?

5) Has anyone in the community tried to do an idea similar to yours, but failed? (Make sure to ask around to see if your idea has been tried before).

Step 3: Complete Market Research

Okay so you've decided on a bar theme and it seems like an amazing idea. Let's go over 3 factors that can still cause a great theme to fail.

1) Too much competition in close proximity (we touched on this in the last step).

2) A Bad Location (More on this in *Step 10*).

3) The target population segment either isn't large enough or doesn't exist to support the concept. (Completing some market research now will help us determine this).

Conducting market research for an area helps to evaluate the level of success your bar theme will have. There are basically 2 ways to complete your market research. Either you can hire a market research company or you can complete your own market research. Whatever option you choose is okay, however, hiring a market research company can get expensive and with a paper and pen we can get this done together.

Remember the 10 mile area that you identified in *Step 2* for where you might want to open a bar? Keep that area in mind as you go through the following 2 parts of your market research.

Part 1: Analyze Population Demographics

So what type of customers do you plan on targeting? 21-35 year olds? 40-60 year olds? Upper class? Middle class? There are no right or wrong answers here. Try to picture what group your bar's theme will attract and let's see what their presence is like in the area. Even if you've lived in an area for years, you might be surprised at what you can learn about the local population so don't skip this step! Find the area's population breakdown by visiting the websites in the ONLINE RESOURCES at the end of this section and completing a search for your city.

By researching the population demographics in an area you can confirm that the population segment you want to attract actually exists and is large enough to support business. You should find out what age ranges have the largest populations, as well as the average age, and population breakdown by gender. It's also important to know the population breakdown of residents versus nonresidents. For example if you want to open a night club in a town where the population segment of 18-25 year olds is scarce and it's not in an area with an influx of young visitors then I predict you're probably setting yourself up for a big failure. The city reports will not only give you insight into the age breakdown of the population, but also data regarding the average income per person and household, as well as employment information. All of this info will help you further analyze whether or not your concept and location have the potential for success. For example if you want to open a wine or martini bar and serve high priced drinks, but the subset of upper class, high earners is practically non-existent then I'd probably rethink my bar theme or find a different area. I'm not saying you couldn't make some money from catering to a very small population segment, but wouldn't you rather be on the safer side and find bigger numbers? Let someone else take the risk of catering to the smaller population segment.

Part 2. Analyze the Competition

So who exactly are your competitors? Your competitors are the bars within 10 miles that have a similar theme or concept to yours. If you have competitors you must pay at least one visit (or more favorably) to their establishments to complete the next part of our market research.

Studying the competition will help give you ideas of how you need to set up and run your bar. Visit their establishments, talk to their customers and staff members, study their ads and press releases, and read their reviews. You want to discover their strengths and weaknesses so you can provide the community with something they lack.

The best part about doing your own research is the cost. All you need is a few dollars to buy a drink or 2 at your competitor's bar, then sit back and observe what's going on around you. You are working here so be careful with downing the dirty martinis. Think about passing up an alcoholic drink for a Coke or an iced tea instead. If you feel like a dweeb taking your pen and paper in with you, just make sure you write down notes as soon as you get back into the car or just take notes on your phone if you have the capability.

Pro Tip: The time of day or week can affect your experience so try visiting once during happy hour on a weekday then maybe come back again late in the evening on a Friday and/or Saturday. The time of year you visit might also affect your research. Summer business versus winter business can vary drastically as well as business around the holidays. Make sure you take the timing of your visit into consideration!

Complete the following questions for each competitor in your area.   If you really feel that no bars in the area are in direct competition with you then analyze 2 or 3 bars (within the 10 miles of where you want to build) that target the same population subset that you want to go after.

Competitor Analysis

Answer these questions for each of your competitors:

1) What are the positive and negatives of their location?

2) What is the atmosphere of their establishment like? (i.e. upscale, relaxed, etc.)

3) Who are their customers? (Take a look around the establishment).

4) What do they offer product wise? Anything unique?

5) What aspects are they really succeeding at?

6) What aspects could they change and improve on?

7) What is the range of pricing for their products? (Ask for a paper menu to take with you to keep as a reference).

8) What are their hours of business? How many hours per day? How many days per week?

9) Do they offer any special promotions during the day or week?

10) What time of the day and/or week are they busiest? If it's due to special promotions, ask what they are? (Ask the bartender or waitress for feedback).

11) Would you come to this bar again? Why or why not?

12) What means do they use to advertise?

In Conclusion…

After you answer these questions for a few of your competitors you should have a better picture of how you would like your bar to look and operate. Try to emulate your competitions strengths while improving on their weak areas. For example, if one of your competitors offers great customer service and has a crowded happy hour with excellent promotions then try to match them in those areas. On the flip side though, maybe the bar area is filthy, they don't offer any entertainment to attract a late night crowd, and they stop serving food at 10pm. This is a great time to learn where your competitors are lacking and figure out ways to outperform them.

ONLINE RESOURCES:

1) Research population demographics:
http://www.census.gov
Use this government hosted site to look up pertinent population information to help you conduct your market research.

http://www.city-data.com
Another great website to find population stats regarding income, education, employment, and age of residents in the area where you would like to start a bar.

Step 4: Set Goals

If you are serious about succeeding, you should always be looking for ways to improve your business and outperform the competition. I'm a big believer that writing down goals creates a roadmap for future success. Since you have finished your market analysis in *Step 3* and the experience is still fresh in your mind, go on to complete a list of goals for the key elements of your establishment.

Pro Tip: When I'm setting goals for a new bar, I find it extremely helpful to visit popular establishments in other cities that have similar themes. This usually helps me gain some design and operational insights as well as inspiration for elements to incorporate in my own bar. For example, before I started building my German Bar and Restaurant, I took an overnight trip to a town four hours away that had a few successful, authentic German restaurants and taverns. I can't tell you how much it helped me in further developing my ideas. I came back from my trip with decorating, set-up, and menu ideas that really helped make my bar successful.

For each of the following goals, brainstorm some unique ideas that you would like to incorporate into your bar. Try and visualize what you would like your bar to look and feel like. Using a country bar theme, I have included some examples below for each goal.

I. Bar Name (Think of a few options and get some feedback from friends. To help with your brainstorming, remember that the name can hint at the theme of your bar or even evoke a certain thought or reaction from the customer. Either way the bar name should appeal to customers and be easy to remember).
Ex: Rodeo Junction, Spurs, Midnight Showdown.

1)

2)

3)

4)

5)

II. Bar Appearance (What will you incorporate into your set-up and/or décor?)
Ex: Rustic looking bar with high wooden chairs, satellite "cowboy shot" bar (with only jager, whiskey, and gin), staff members must wear cowboy hats, jeans/jean shorts, boots.

1)

2)

3)

4)

5)

III. Bar Ambiance (How do you want your customers to feel in your establishment?)
Ex: During the Day and Evening: Informal, Relaxed, Leisurely. During night: Lively, Loud, and Social.

1)

2)

3)

4)

5)

IV. Entertainment (What will you provide in terms of TV/music/games?)
Ex: Country music with country bands on weekends, pool tables, Thursday through Saturday staff members dance on bar.

1)

2)

3)

4)

5)

V. Customer Service (How will your management/staff provide excellent service?)

Ex: Customers greeted upon entry and exit, drink orders taken within first minute of seating, manager meets and greets customers throughout night to check on service quality of staff and promote business

1)

2)

3)

4)

5)

VI. Promotions (What daily/weekly product specials or unique promotional events will you offer?)
Ex: Karaoke country night with prizes, "Ladies night" where girls in cowboy boots get $1 drinks, "Cowboy night" with $2 shots from cowboy bar

1)

2)

3)

4)

5)

VII. Products (What will your top menu items include?)
Ex: Buckets of beer, mini beef barbeque sliders, big burgers, chicken wings, "Wild West" beer (32oz mug).

1)

2)

3)

4)

5)

Step 5: Form a Corporation

Forming a corporation or other business entity for your bar is absolutely necessary. The process has never cost me more than $100, so you really don't have any excuse (other than laziness) for not taking care of this immediately. Not having a business entity will slow you down when you continue to other steps, so get it done now!

Having a corporation or business entity can:

- Help you obtain licenses (in certain states).
- Provide protection from your personal assets should there be any legal issues down the road.
- Keep your personal and business accounts separate for accounting and tax reasons.
- Provide certain tax benefits and write-offs.
- Show that you are professional and motivated when you go to obtain financing, because lenders or potential partners can see that you are serious about getting your business started.

There are many types of entities you can form for your business. Personally I prefer forming Limited Liability Companies (LLCs) because of the tax benefits and because I usually only have one other business partner involved. Don't worry about waiting to create a business entity after you find partners or investors, because you can always add them into the documents down the road.

Let's go over the most common corporate and business entities you may form for your business as well as the positives and/or negatives of each. Please note that some of the entities may not be available in your specific state.

1) Sole Proprietorship (business entity)
A sole proprietorship is the most basic form of business ownership and brings major disadvantages for bar business owners. If the business experiences financial difficulties, creditors of the business can seek and attach the owner's personal property; therefore, your personal credit can be negatively affected. On the positive side the sole owner does not have to pay corporate taxes, but self-employment taxes and the owner never has to worry about double taxation. Sole proprietorships are very easy to set up, but I would never go this route when starting a bar because of the lack of personal protection.

2) Partnership (business entity)
A general partnership consists of two or more people, where each person is responsible for their own actions as well as the actions of the other partner(s).

All partners are personally responsible for debt assumed on behalf of the business, no matter which partner brought on the debt. Once an individual contributes assets to the business, personal ownership of the assets is lost, because the assets become equity of the business. Partnerships are sometimes favored over corporations for taxation purposes because generally there is not tax on profits before they are distributed to the partners.

3) Limited Partnership (business entity)
A limited partnership is similar to a general partnership (see above), however the partners in a limited partnership are only liable for the amount personally invested in the business. Limited partnerships are more common if you are going to buy the actual real estate of the bar with partners.

4) Limited Liability Company (business entity)
A Limited Liability Company (LLC) has features of a partnership and corporation. An LLC provides its owners with limited liability, which means that each individual member is protected from some or all liability of acts and debts of the LLC depending on state laws. LLC's also have the choice to be taxed as a sole proprietor, partnership, S corporation, or C corporation, which offers greater taxation flexibility. A disadvantage to forming LLC's is that some states (AL, CA, KY, NY, PA, TN, TX) add franchise tax or capital values tax onto LLC's Also if you are in Washington, D.C. they consider LLC's to be a taxable entity and they subject members to double taxation.

5) Corporation (corporate entity)
A corporation is a separate entity from the owner(s) and therefore, is only legally responsible for the actions and debt of the business. If the corporation experiences financial difficulties, creditors of the business can seek and attach the shareholders' personal property and negatively affect personal credit. Another disadvantage of a corporation is double taxation because the corporation must pay taxes on net income, and the shareholders must pay taxes on dividends received. Also expect a greater amount of paperwork and documentation then say an LLC. If you are thinking about raising capital and selling shares of ownership to investors, you might want to consider starting a corporation because most investors are more comfortable with a corporate business structure.

6) S Corporation (corporate entity)
An S Corporation does not pay taxes on its income. Rather, the income and expenses are divided among shareholders who must report them on their personal income tax returns. The major disadvantage of an S Corporation is that the number of shareholders is usually limited to a certain number.

How to Form a Business Entity

To form a business entity you can hire an attorney or you can use an online company if you know what entity you want to form. The bonus of forming a corporation online is that you won't get hit with expensive attorney fees, extra charges, and you'll also save time by not having to leave your office. If you decide to hire an attorney make sure you find one who specializes in setting up business entities for people in the bar restaurant industry. Don't forget to inquire about their rates before you schedule a meeting. I'd recommend calling 3 attorneys before you make your final decision.

Pro Tip: Even if you want to set up a business entity on-line it doesn't hurt to develop a relationship with an attorney whom you can e-mail or call from time to time should any legal questions come up.

Employer ID Number

After you form a business entity you need to obtain an Employer ID number (EIN). The EIN is also known as the Federal Tax Identification number. The IRS uses the number to identify taxpayers that are required to file various business tax returns. Once you have legally formed a corporate entity you can go on the IRS's website to use their free online application for your EIN (see site address below). Even if you plan on using an accountant, it isn't a bad idea to spend some extra time on the IRS's website getting acquainted with the different tax rules for restaurants and bars. Look in the ONLINE RESOURCES below for how to get to the portion of the IRS's site that deals directly with the restaurant industry.

ONLINE RESOURCES:

1) Form a business entity:
http://www.legalzoom.com
Use this site to form a business entity without even leaving your office.

2) Apply for an EIN:
https://sa1.www4.irs.gov/modiein/individual/index.jsp
Use this site to begin your application process for an EIN. It's free and you should have an EIN within a few weeks. Make sure you form a corporation before you apply.

Step 6: Estimate Startup Costs and Create a Business Plan

It's nearly impossible to know the exact amount of money needed to open a bar, but all you need is a general estimate. This estimate will not only give you a dollar amount to aim for, but also a number you can relay to bankers and potential investors when trying to find financing. Anyone who might provide a loan or invest money in your business absolutely needs to see that you have done your research. Before we get into estimating startup costs let's discuss 2 choices you can make early that have the power to dramatically reduce your costs before you even start.

1) Plan on opening a Smaller Bar.

A smaller bar means a lower security deposit, monthly rent payment, smaller deposits for electric/gas/water as well as monthly bills, less equipment/supply costs, lower insurance, and less payroll…..sounds better, doesn't it?

Another way to reduce startup costs is to….

2) Plan on opening a bar in a space previously used as a bar or restaurant.

Finding a space that was a bar or restaurant means less work and less money out of your pocket. Normally a space previously used as a bar or restaurant already has the basics that you need in regards to bathrooms and kitchens being up to code, as well as plumbing and electricity already hooked up as needed. If you don't choose a space that was a bar or restaurant, plan on forking out a lot more dough and spending more time to get in the game. Deciding to renovate a space and bring it up to code will easily double if not triple your costs.

Main Startup Costs

I have built enough bars over the years, so I can pretty much eyeball a commercial space and get an accurate estimate as to how much it's going to cost me to open a bar. If you are new to this business you won't have that same luxury, so I recommend spending more time doing the necessary work to analyze possible expenses. Unfortunately, I can't tell you how much money it should cost you, because it really depends on your concept, your area, and the lease space you wind up with. Let's research the following expenses and see what you come up with.

1) Security Deposit / Rent
Hopefully you can negotiate some build out time in your lease, so you can have 1-3 months of no rent payments while your bar is under construction. Regardless, you still must be prepared to pay a security deposit to secure the contract.

Call around to get a feel for the average cost per square foot of commercial space in the area you want to rent. If you want more square footage, you better be ready to pay more.

2) Equipment *(See Steps 12 & 16)*
Equipment can get extremely expensive, especially if you plan on pumping out a lot of food. In that case, you can easily spend $30k on kitchen equipment like ovens, prep stations, ansul system ($5k-$10k), grease trap, deep fryer, refrigerators, ice machines, and freezers. Now can you see why I like building smaller bars without a huge focus on food? I always win in the long run because I reduce start up costs and focus more on selling the products with the highest profit margins….drinks!

Equipment isn't only for food and drink preparation either. Don't overlook the cost of all the other equipment you need like TVs, sound system, bar equipment, tables, and seating.

3) Licenses / Permits *(See Step 10)*
Obtaining licenses and permits to build your bar and open to the public can be very costly. Liquor licenses especially can get expensive and can range anywhere from a few hundred dollars to over $100k depending on where you open your bar. License and permit applications also take time to process, which means you might have to incur other costs in the meantime if you can't open your doors to the public. You should definitely do your research early in the game as to what your state and county requires in terms of different permits and licenses, as well as how much time they take to obtain and how much they cost.

4) Insurance *(See Step 10)*

5) Alarm System / Cameras *(See Step 14)*

6) Electricity, Gas, Water (deposits and bills for first few months)
Deposits are easy to overlook, but a lot of companies require a deposit before they provide service. You also need to plan on paying for the first few bills out of pocket, while you get the bar ready for opening.

7) Construction Costs *(See Step 15)*

8) Services- Trash, Cable or Satellite, Internet (installation/deposits and bills for the first few months**)** *(See Step 16)*

9) Decorations and Signage *(See Step 13)*

10) First Couple Inventory Orders (Food, Liquor, Beer, and Wine) *(See Step 18)*

11) Supplies *(See Steps 12 & 16)*
Don't forget about all the little things that you need to buy like towels, toilet paper, and cleaning supplies. Some states allow employers to charge employees for uniforms, so depending on where you live you might not have to come out of pocket for uniforms.

12) Payroll, Taxes
Even in the first few weeks of opening you will have expenses that your business may not be able to cover. I recommend being prepared to pay for payroll and taxes out of pocket just in case. Some tax bills come quarterly and some come monthly (depends on your state), but either way it's an expense you need to be aware of and ready to pay.

And the Total is........

Total the above 12 expenses then add 20-30% on top. This final number should give you the amount of money you need (including a little cushion) to open comfortably. Now don't freak out about the total if you don't have all the necessary cash, we are going to talk more in *Step 7* about ways to find and use OPM (Other People's Money)....the best type of money there is!

Create a Business Plan

Before you run off trying to find financing or a lease, you need to put together a business plan first. A business plan is going to show the mission of your business, what you are providing the community with, and a breakdown of your startup costs. Of course this will most likely change a great deal after you get started, but your main goal now is to get organized and have something to present when looking for financing.

When creating your business plan remember to:

- Keep your plan well organized and not too lengthy. Even 2-4 pages will be enough.
- Make it clear and logical. Have others proofread your plan to make sure it makes sense.
- Keep it professional and appealing to the eye. Always type your business plan and make sure to put a presentation cover on each copy you hand out.
- Update your plan should you make any changes.

- Format the document in outline form. No need to write paragraph after paragraph.

Sections to include in your bar business plan are:

I.   **Mission** – Give the name of your establishment and theme.

II.   **Objective** – Explain what your establishment will provide to the community (i.e. job creation, entertainment, increased popularity of area).

III.   **Market Analysis** – Prove the need for your establishment in the area by addressing issues affecting the market (i.e. growing population, new developments, etc.). Include the population subset your establishment will target.

IV.   **Strategy and Implementation Summary** – Include a brief summary for the course of action you will take to get up and running. You can always summarize the steps I'm giving you now (easy enough, right).

V.   **Products** - List 10 items that you plan to serve on your menu. You just need some rough ideas for now and later in *Step 18* you can finalize a menu.

VI.   **Startup Costs** – Show the breakdown of estimated expenses we calculated earlier in this section.

VII.   **Closing** – Sum up why you are going to be extremely successful. Go ahead and brag about your past accomplishments!

ONLINE RESOURCES:

1) Write your business plan:
http://www.bplans.com/sample_business_plans.cfm
Here you can look at some sample business plans for free. Some are quite extensive, but they will help give you an idea of what to aim for.

http://www.sba.gov/smallbusinessplanner/plan/writeabusinessplan/ index.html
A great source for tips on how to write your business plan.

Step 7: Figure out Financing and Banking

If you have the money to finance your business and still have enough money left over to live comfortably until you start making profits then great! You however, are in the minority. Even if you have the money you might want to consider finding financing or investors, so you don't have to go into your stash of savings. I've always tried to use OPM in my businesses. OPM stands for Other People's Money and it's the best way to leverage your money and make bigger money faster. If you like the sound of OPM and want to learn more I recommend you read the books in Robert Kiyosaki's Rich Dad Advisor Series called, "Rich Dad Poor Dad" and "OPM: How to Attract Other People's Money for Your Investments—The Ultimate Leverage." Now let's go over some options to find some funding for your bar.

Major Items Needed for Funding

1) Business Plan (See *Step 6* for more information)
Anytime you apply for funding you must have a business plan ready. You will appear unprofessional and unprepared without one.

2) Business Pro Forma- A business pro forma estimates future earnings potential. Hire an accountant that has experience in creating pro formas to help you with this document and include it with your business plan. Spend some extra time with your accountant so you understand what everything means, so you can explain and present it to other interested parties. If you apply for bank loans or sba loans a pro forma is usually mandatory. Even potential investors could ask for a pro forma, so it can't hurt to have one done.

Finding Financial Funding

The bar business is considered a high-risk investment, but that doesn't mean you won't be able to find funding. Some possible avenues to explore include:
1) Bank Loans
2) SBA Loans
3) Angel Investors
4) Venture Capitalist
5) Promissory Notes
6) Finding a Bar Owner Who Wants Out of An Existing Establishment
7) Finding a Desperate Landlord Who Offers Money for a Profitable Tenant
8) Equity Companies
9) Friends and Family Members
10) Partnerships

11) Selling Shares to Investors

Pro Tip: Watch the "Figuring Out Financing" DVD included in my program. This DVD reviews all of the means of finding financing from the previous list.

Before Obtaining Funding

If you are receiving money from investors or partners don't even think of spending a dime until everything promised is in your possession. I know this sounds ridiculously basic, but I've heard too many stories of owners who spent thousands on their own credit cards expecting to be reimbursed by investors, only to have the deal fall through.

Set-Up Banking

When you have your funding lined up start looking for a bank in your area. You must have your Employer Identification Number (discussed in *Step 5*) to open a business bank account, so make sure you have this before you start visiting banks in the area.

Some key issues to pay attention to:
- Minimum balance required
- Transaction fees / Account maintenance fees
- Interest earned on balance
- Proximity to your bar's area. This is important because you or your manager must make frequent trips to make deposits.

Open a Credit Card for Business

Opening a business credit card isn't always necessary, but it's a great chance to earn major points on travel and other rewards. Personally, I like American Express, but it's worth checking different cards to see what suits you best. Make sure to pay at least your minimum payment each month. Building good credit and keeping good credit is a huge deal, so make this a priority going forward.

I advise you to use extreme caution on trusting your business debit card, checks, or credit card with anyone but yourself. If you do, make sure you get receipts and check balances on a regular basis. If you allow a manager to have access to the checks or credit card, set rules on what charges they must ask permission for, as well as what they are allowed to purchase. Personally, I never allowed any staff members to use my debit or credit card, but I know other owners that do and it works for them. I leave the final decision to your discretion.

ONLINE RESOURCES:

1) Open a business credit card:
http://www.creditcards.com/business.php
With this site you can browse through different card offers with ease and submit applications online. Even if you don't have the best credit do a "Search by Credit Quality" located on the left menu bar to see what's available to you.

Step 8: Find a Location

Before you start looking for real estate you should know how much you want to spend and whether or not you would like to lease or buy. Buying might be a good investment for the future, but if you end up disliking the business or have financial problems then it's a lot more difficult to walk away. Another problem with owning is that there is always a slight possibility that a license or permit could fall through and you aren't allowed to open, then what do you do? Leasing property gives you a little more breathing room. Personally, I always seek out leases, because it gives me more flexibility.

Finding a lease with an option to buy can give you the best of both worlds. This way you have some time to create a viable business before you purchase the real estate, plus you won't suffer any penalties should you choose not to buy. Another advantage of a lease purchase is that it enables you to lock in a purchase price ahead of time. Obviously, this works out great when the purchase price is considerably below the market value when you go to exercise the option.

Dealing With Landlords

When you start calling about properties, landlords will ask you what kind of business you plan on starting. Now one thing I've learned after years of opening bars is NEVER TELL THE LANDLORD YOU ARE OPENING A BAR. Now just hear me out! I know it sounds strange, but I've dealt with a lot of landlords in my day. Landlords (and most of the general public) have the perception that a bar means total chaos and destruction with loud music, drunk people running around, people puking in the parking lot, drug use going on in the bathrooms, and beer bottles everywhere. The average landlord really doesn't want to take that much risk with their investment, would you?

Now, I don't want you to lie, but I DO want you to downplay the "bar" part. When you are talking with a landlord, say that you are opening a "restaurant and bar", "grille and bar", or "bistro and bar". Notice how I include "bar" at the end of each name? We want the landlord to think that the "bar" part is an afterthought, not the main attraction. If you tell a landlord that you are opening a bar, I guarantee most landlords are going to find some excuse not to lease you their space. This isn't always true of all landlords, but why take a chance and miss out on a great lease space that could potentially be absolutely perfect for your business? I rest my case.

Where to Find Commercial property:

- Internet (See ONLINE RESOURCES)
- Drive around your area and look for property
- Local Newspaper
- Find a real estate agent who deals with commercial property

Location Factors

One of the most important and costly decisions will be finding an ideal location. A bad location can ruin your business even if you have a terrific concept. Go back to the 10 mile area that you analyzed in your market research and search for some available real estate to take a closer look at.

Pro Tip: Watch the "Finding a Successful Location" DVD in my program where I show you exactly how I analyze property.

Location factors to consider:
- Distance from main roads: Can the property be easily found and accessed? Are there barriers such as traffic congestion or frequent road construction that might affect business?
- Distance from competitors: A distance of 10 miles from direct competition is safe, but proximity to other popular bars actually helps gain business from bar hoppers.
- Area's population demographics: Does the location target the kind of customer you want to attract?
- Distance from high crime areas: Unnecessary trouble should always be avoided.
- Highly trafficked area: Are there other popular shops or restaurants close by?
- Total monthly/yearly costs.
- Square footage: How big do you want your bar to be?
- Number of seats: To obtain a liquor license in some states you must fit a certain number of seats.
- Costly necessities available: Is there an existing bar, proper electrical wiring, water heater, and/or AC/Heater.
- Bathrooms up to current health codes (this can get very expensive).
- Adequate Customer Parking.
- Sign Placement: Can you put adequate signage up or are there limitations?
- Construction Costs: How much work are you going to have to do? Are the floors/ceiling/walls in decent shape? How much will you have to spend on renovations? Will the landlord chip in?

- Zoning Laws: Don't assume that just because the previous tenant opened a bar that you're allowed to open one up too....laws change.

- Grease trap present: If your state requires you to serve food the Health Department may require you to have a grease trap, which can cost anywhere from $1,500 to $10,000.
- Hood and Ansul systems present: These systems are required if you are cooking food and they can run around $10,000.

Pro Tip: Fill out the "Location Analysis" worksheet for every property you go see. This worksheet will help you remember the most important factors when opening a bar and help you compare properties against each other. The "Location Analysis" worksheet is located in the *Additional Resources* section in the back of this manual.

Look for Space previously used as a Bar or Restaurant

Like I said before, it's always best to find real estate property that was previously used as a bar or restaurant, because your startup costs will be significantly lower. Typically there should be less construction and remodeling then if you were starting from complete scratch. If you build from scratch you will have to go through the hassle of bringing the space up to current health and safety codes, which is extremely costly and takes considerably more time.

Why Bigger is NOT Always Better

When figuring how much square footage you need, remember that bigger is not always better. People want to be around a party when they go out, so if you have a larger sized bar you will need more customers present for the impression of a lively atmosphere. In comparison, a smaller bar can have an energetic feel with far fewer customers. And remember, energetic bars are popular bars and popular bars translate to more profits.

Analyze Expenses

Once you find a property that appeals to you, spend some time trying to figure out what the expenses run. I always find out about the water, electric, and insurance bills as well as estimating how much the construction will cost me. I usually get quotes from contractors in this stage to see if I can afford what needs to be done.

I once wanted to lease a new building that was only a shell and didn't have any plumbing or electric installed yet. It was a fantastic location, so I researched what it would cost me to build out. I got on the phone and started to call everyone I could to find out about the total expenses. Everything checked out okay until I came across the water department. They told me that I would be charged an "impact fee" for putting in new plumbing and I would pay based on however many seats I would have in the bar.   I told them I would have 40 seats and they told me I would be charged around $40,000! Wow, that took the breadth right out of my chest! I was planning to spend less than $80k on the entire project and that was almost going to double my budget. Needless to say I found a different spot to lease.

ONLINE RESOURCES:

1) Look for available commercial property:
http://www.Craigslist.org
Depending on the area, some property owners use Craigslist to post their commercial listings.

http://www.Loopnet.com
This is a fairly new site that specializes in commercial property listings.

Step 9: Negotiate the Lease

Negotiating the lease is a very crucial process. Basically it has the potential to either make or break you. Landlords need somebody to pay them rent and you want the best deal you can get, so take the bull by the horns and ask for what you want. The same goes for property on sale (if you go that route). Never settle for the first price they ask for. ALWAYS negotiate, negotiate, and negotiate some more. If you don't feel comfortable negotiating then find a Realtor who specializes in commercial real estate to negotiate on your behalf. Having a realtor guide you through the process won't cost you a penny. The landlord is the one responsible for paying the realtor's commission so don't worry about having to spend any extra money in this department.

I hate to bring it up, but I must warn you that landlords can be a real pain to deal with in the beginning. Every landlord I've ever met has some sort of sob story about how badly they've been burned by a tenant in the past. Unfortunately you will have to go in and "disarm" their negative attitude, so to speak. Come up with ways to make the landlord feel comfortable with you as a tenant. Always act respectful and feel free to present any written evidence of your past business successes that show that you are professional as well as motivated. This along with always paying your rent on time will help you develop a better business relationship along the way.

You might run into problems obtaining a lease if you have bad credit, no experience, and/or if you are young and fairly new to the business world. You can do 2 things to combat these issues if they apply to you. First, find a successful family member or friend to cosign with you and second you must always present yourself as extremely professional and business oriented in the way you dress and interact.

Negotiations can take a couple of days to months depending on the location and the current economy, so don't be surprised if this process takes longer than you originally thought. Also, there are plenty of properties out there so don't become emotionally attached to any particular space. Always mentally prepare yourself to walk away from the deal if the terms are more than you budgeted for.

Pro Tip: I always negotiate multiple properties at the same time to keep things moving. This also gives me leverage to negotiate one landlord against another. Most of the time if I'm working on three deals at once, only one ends up working out in the end anyway.

Considerations to include in the lease:
- Duration of lease: Something between 3-5 years is ideal.
- Option to renew: At the end of the lease term (3-5 years) you want the option to stay there if you choose to. An option to renew means that you have a choice (no matter what) to renew or to walk away without penalty. I always negotiate around 12-15 years of options to renew.
- Option to buy (if it's a lease purchase): At the end of the lease term (3-5 years) you have an option to exercise your right to buy the property at a certain set price.
- 2-3 Months Build Out time: I always negotiate for this, because it gives me time to set up my bar without paying rent. Sometimes I only get 1-2 months, but it's better than nothing. Your landlord should want you to succeed, and if you are paying rent with no money coming in, it's going to be hard. You still must pay a security deposit first, so don't expect to get out of that.
- Statement that declares you enter into the lease agreement under the pretense that the space is up to Health, Safety, and Fire Codes and that if any costs arise the landlord is responsible. That way if there are costly repairs or changes cited by an inspector, you can get the landlord to fix things, because it would mean a breach of the lease.
- Repairs: Have the landlord fix as much as possible before you start to put your money to work.
- Tenant improvement concessions: See if the landlord will agree to a yearly tenant improvement allowance that would enable you to make yearly repairs on the building (these are hard to come by, but why not ask).
- Contingency clause that states the contract is null and void if any of your permits or licenses (liquor, building, and/or business) fall through or are revoked. **A MUST HAVE!**

Pro Tip: The last item on the list is extremely important because if the county or city puts a block on your business, you will legally be allowed to get out of the contract. This clause saved me big time in the past. I once tried to open a bar and after I signed the lease the town denied my business license application. Town regulations would not allow two bars within 500 feet of each other and since there was another bar close by they couldn't allow me to build another. So there I was with a signed lease, renovations about to begin, and I couldn't get approved for a business license.   Luckily the lawyers were able to work things out and we got out of the lease. I still lost about $6,000 of deposit money, but that was still better than having to pay out a few years of lease money if we defaulted.

Also, don't be afraid to ask the landlord to make structural changes. If there is a major issue with the set-up holding you back from the deal then tell the landlord and see what they have to say. Sometimes they need a tenant so badly, they will do just about anything to make the deal happen. For example I once looked at a lease space with a drop down ceiling, which left nowhere for smoke to vent to. This would have been a huge issue because the bar would fill with smoke faster and people would not want to hang around. Lucky for me, the landlord agreed to rip out the drop ceiling and prime everything on his own coin, which saved me an easy $10k.

Pro Tip: If you don't already have one, locate a business attorney in town. Set up a sit down introductory meeting with a few attorneys (make sure they are not going to charge you for this). The purpose of the meeting is to introduce yourself, tell them that you are new in the business, and let them know you would like to avoid any problems early. Ask them if you would be able to call or e-mail them should any questions come up. This business relationship will help you get questions answered quickly and also help if any lawsuits surface. Get in the habit of having an attorney review every contract before you sign. Don't rely on a real estate agent to know the correct wordage and legalities.

Phase 1: Pre-Bar Summary
Complete Steps in Order

Step 1: Gut Check
- Before getting into this business you need to make sure you are 100% ready to do what it takes to succeed.
- Prepare your loved ones for what's in store.
- Analyze where you are with your savings and whether or not you have enough saved away to support yourself while you get your bar up and running.
- Figure out whether you are prepared to run bar operations by yourself or whether you will spend money on a full time manager.

Step 2: Choose a Theme
- Identify a 10-mile area where you would like to start a bar.
- Determine what market niche isn't being filled in the area.
- Know what concept you want to incorporate for your bar as well as what customer demographics you want to target.
- To be as profitable as possible, your bar should offer the community something it does not currently have.

Step 3: Complete Market Research
- Market research will either confirm or dispel your theme idea.
- You need to analyze the area's population demographics (age and income level) to see if the target area supports your concept.
- Get acquainted with your competitors to learn their strengths and weaknesses, so you know how you need to operate.
- Competitors are bars within 10 miles away that have similar themes.
- If you don't have competitors then analyze the bars in the area that target the same population demographic that you plan to target.

Step 4: Set Goals
- Goals are necessary for success and are much more effective when you write them down.
- Goals can change, but they should give you a blueprint to follow and come back to.
- You should set goals and brainstorm ideas for your Bar's Name, Bar Appearance/Ambiance, Entertainment, Customer Service, Promotions, and Products.

Step 5: Form a Corporation

- Not forming a corporate or business entity early can hold you back in future steps (i.e. obtaining certain permits/licenses)
- Business entities and corporations protect personal assets, keep business accounting separate, as well as provide tax benefits.
- You can form a legal entity online or you can go through an attorney.
- After you form a legal entity, file for an EIN through the IRS's website.

Step 6: Estimate Startup Costs and Create a Business Plan
- Startup costs differ between bars but opening a smaller bar and choosing a lease space that was previously used as a bar or restaurant can drastically reduce startup costs.
- The major startup costs that you need to research in your area are security deposits/rent, equipment, licenses/permits, insurance, alarm system/cameras, electricity/gas/water deposits and bills for first few months, construction costs, first few months of services (garbage, satellite TV, internet), decorations/signage, first few food/alcohol inventory orders, supplies, and payroll/taxes.
- After you total your startup costs add 20-30% on top to factor in a cushion, so you can open comfortably.
- A business plan not only keeps you organized, but conveys to others that you mean business.
- Present a business plan when trying to secure financing with a bank or recruit investors.
- A business plan only needs to be a few pages long.

Step 7: Figure out Financing and Banking
- Use OPM (Other People's Money) whenever possible.
- Watch the DVD in my program called "Figuring Out Financing" for more information.
- Possible avenues for financing your bar include bank loans, SBA loans, angel investors, venture capitalist, promissory notes, finding a bar owner who wants out of an existing establishment, finding a desperate landlord who offers money for a profitable tenant, equity companies, friends and family members, partnerships, and/or selling shares to investors.
- Open a separate bank account for your business as well as a separate credit card.

Step 8: Find a Location
- Figure out whether you want to lease or buy the real estate for your bar.
- Leases give more flexibility should a problem arise.
- A lease with an option to purchase gives the flexibility of a lease, but also gives the option to buy the real estate at a predetermined time in the future if so desired.

A landlord might turn you down for a lease if you tell them you are opening a bar. Try and downplay the "bar" part by saying "grille and bar,"

- "restaurant and bar," or "bistro and bar."
- Go back to the 10-mile area you completed your market research on and look at properties.
- Use the "Location Analysis" worksheet in the *Additional Resources* section to analyze every property you view.

Step 9: Negotiate the Lease

- Always negotiate the lease to work for you and prepare yourself to walk away if things don't go the way you want.
- Act professional in every way when dealing with the landlord.
- Sometimes negotiating is a lengthy process, so negotiating a few contracts at once may help you get the deal you want, faster.
- Include the following considerations in your lease: duration of lease, option to renew, 2-3 months build out time, statement confirming building is up to all codes, repairs to building that landlord will make, tenant improvement concessions, and a contingency clause that declares contract is null and void if permits or licenses fall through.
- Always have an attorney review your final lease before you sign.

Phase 2:
Pre-Construction

Attack Steps Simultaneously

Step 10: Obtain Permits, Licenses, and Insurance

The permits and licenses required to open your bar will differ depending on your county and state. Every area has different "hoops" to jump through (so to speak) to get your bar up and running. Besides contacting the local and state authorities to find out about the requirements, also speak with a few local bar owners and ask them what permits and licenses they acquired to open.

Let's go over 3 of the most common licenses and permits that bar owners usually need. These include the business license, building permit, and liquor license.

Business License

As I mentioned earlier, most people have a very negative perception of the bar business. That's why you need to be very careful using the word "bar" when trying to obtain a business license or other permit from a city department. Most cities probably won't have a problem, but there definitely are others that do (believe me I've dealt with them) and they will do whatever it takes to keep you from getting the necessary licenses to operate. Just like I explained earlier in *Step 8*, I'm not telling you to change your concept. You just have to finesse your plan a little by using a description like "restaurant and bar," "grille and bar," "bistro and bar," or alternative wordage that downplays the "bar" part.

Building Permit

Before you begin construction you need to have the correct permits. You must talk to someone in your city's building department to see what they require of you before beginning construction. Some cities require you to build certain amenities to get up to code (i.e. handicap bathrooms or handicap sections of the bar). Talking to the building department early will give you a good game plan for how you need to proceed.

The complicated part about obtaining building permits is that every city has different requirements and some are definitely crazier than others. One time I was waiting for permission to renovate a 1200 sq. ft lease space even though I wasn't doing any major construction. Since the rental space was located in a shopping plaza that was over 5,000 sq. ft., there was a crazy city rule that stated I was required to submit architecture drawings for approval. I had to hire an architect for $1,000 and have them draw up plans before I was allowed to even put paint on the walls. Talk about annoying rules.

Some city building departments want to know what your budget is for your renovations. If your construction budget falls under a certain number, let's say $5,000, then they may allow you to get by with submitting your own floor plans without hiring an architect (which can get expensive).

I usually choose lease spots that do not need much construction other than maybe building a bar, cleaning, and decorating. That being said, most of the time I get away with submitting my own floor plans. If the building department allows you to submit a floor plan on your own then go buy some graph paper from Walmart or Staples, measure your bar's floor plan dimensions, and plot out the bar's layout. Make sure you also include the measurements on the graph paper.

Liquor License

Depending on your state and/or county, obtaining a liquor license can sometimes be a tricky and lengthy process. Your State Department of Alcohol regulates the buying and selling of alcohol to the public and this is whom you need to contact to figure out how to obtain a liquor license (for contact information for your state agency responsible for alcohol licenses, laws, and/or control of alcohol please visit the *Additional Resources* section in the back of this manual). Some states (i.e. Florida) are only allowed to issue so many licenses, so you must buy a license from a liquor license broker or enter into a lottery drawing. Other states allow you to apply right away and have a license within a couple of months.

Once you obtain your liquor license, learn the rules and requirements you need to follow in order to keep your license. For example some states require that an establishment must serve food or have a certain number of seats available in order to keep a liquor license. Other states require that the total liquor sales equal a specific percentage of total sales, which means a bar better be pumping out a certain amount of food. The bottom line is that you absolutely need to know your states' requirements and act accordingly, in order to obtain and keep your licenses. If you break liquor license laws you can get hit with some hefty fines and eventually lose your liquor license, which is definitely not what you need.

Also, when you obtain your license don't think that you are automatically allowed to serve beer and wine. Some states, like South Carolina, require you to obtain a separate license.

Know Your Regulations

Each state is different and since time is of the essence, you don't need any last minute surprises. Make sure you find out all there is to know about labor laws, fire and safety codes, food and alcohol regulations, as well as any bylaws regarding advertising for your specific city and state.

Contact each of the following groups to know what they require and/or recommend for doing business in your area:

1) State Bar/Restaurant Association
2) Town/City Hall

3) National Health Department

4) Local Chamber of Commerce

5) State Chamber of Commerce

6) State Department of Alcohol

7) Internal Revenue Service

8) Department of Labor

Find Insurance

Insurance is an absolute necessity to protect your investment and you'll need to find insurance as soon as you take possession of the property. Obtain at least 3 quotes from 3 different insurance companies and be sure to use an insurance agent that has significant experience with commercial insurance. Deciding how much insurance to carry will depend mainly on the probability of a loss as well as the resources you have available to meet that loss. Spending some extra time with the insurance agent to figure this out is highly recommended. Some of the issues that you will need to consider coverage for include:

- Burglary insurance- covering forced entry and theft of merchandise and cash.
- Fidelity bonding- covering theft by an employee.
- Accidents / Injuries:
    Public liability- covering injury to the public such as a customer or pedestrian falling on the property.
    Product liability- covering injury to customers arising from the use of goods purchased through the business.
    Errors and omissions- covering the bar against claims from customers who suffer injury or loss because of errors made, or things that should have been done that were not done.
- Assault
- Consequential loss insurance- covering loss of earnings or extra expenses when business is suspended due to fire or other catastrophe.
- Fire
- Flood

- Plate glass

- Fraud Insurance- covering counterfeit money, bad checks, and larceny as well as stolen credit cards.
- Liquor liability
- Contractual liability
- Advertising liability
- Medical expenses
- Worker's compensation and employers' liability
- Personal Property (Equipment & Supplies)
- Life Insurance- covering the life of the owner(s) or key employee(s).
- Other environmental factors (depending on your area)-hail, wind, earthquake damage.
- Company health insurance for your staff. Obviously you don't have to provide this, but it will make you a more competitive employer. You may want to add this as a benefit after so many months of employment or make it available for upper level positions such as a full time manager.

Pro Tip: As you probably could have guessed, insurance companies don't want to pay out so they place loopholes in the coverage. For example they might state in the policy that all employees and servers must have a training class on how to serve alcohol. Now if something happens and you want to collect on a claim, but don't have proof that the servers completed a training class, the insurance company may find a way out of paying the claim. Insurance companies can also add items in your policy that regulate what time to stop selling alcohol, employee alcohol consumption, or pricing stipulations for beer or liquor. By not fully understanding your policy you can create a lot of costly problems down the road.

ONLINE RESOURCES:

1) Find out what licenses and permits you need for your area:
http://www.business.gov/register/licenses-and-permits/
This website allows you to search for the permits and licenses you need to open a restaurant by entering your zip code. Obviously bars sometimes have different license/permit requirements, but if you plan on serving food then the requirements should be fairly similar. Either way this website will give you a good idea as to what you need to research further.

2) Educate yourself on taxes:
http://www.irs.ustreas.gov/businesses/small/industries/
This is a great site to educate new bar owners about everything you need to know regarding the different taxes you are responsible for. Scroll down and click on "Restaurants Tax Center."

3) Learn about federal regulations:
http://www.business.gov/industries/food/restaurants.html
This site addresses legal and regulatory issues impacting the food and beverage industry. Some important issues that affect your bar are covered on this site, including the Americans with Disabilities Act, child and teen labor, immigration, minimum wage, tips, overtime, and food safety requirements.

4) Find out about your specific state's alcohol laws:
http://en.wikipedia.org/wiki/List_of_alcohol_laws_of_the_United_States_by_state
A summary of key alcohol laws by State.

5) Learn about federal labor laws:
http://www.dol.gov

6) Contact the National Health Department:

Step 11: Schedule Pre-Inspections

Sometimes when you move into a space there will be equipment and supplies left behind from the previous owner or tenant. You have inherited these items, unless it specifically states somewhere in the lease that the items belong to the landlord. Use whatever items you can and try and sell the remainders. Take pictures and post them on Craigslist or in the local newspaper. A little extra cash never hurts!

Pro Tip: Pre-Inspections aren't mandatory by any means, but believe me, after I started doing pre-inspections I found I was able to open bars faster and save more money. I didn't enjoy finding out in the final stages of opening that I needed to rip something out and start over. This costs valuable time and a lot of extra money. I'd rather find out in the beginning, so I set things up the right way. As long as you like saving time and money, which I'm guessing you do, I recommend you schedule pre-inspections too.

Fire Pre-Inspection

Most bar owners schedule the fire marshall to come for a final inspection when they are ready to open. Smart bar owners have the fire marshall come out before construction begins to find out exactly what they need in order to obey fire codes. Walk the fire marshall through your space and go over your core design. Ask them if they see any issues. What do you need in terms of exit signs? Building changes? Fire alarms? Fire extinguishers? What else do you need to prepare for? Do they foresee any occupancy issues?

Getting the fire marshall into your bar pre-construction will do two things for you. First, you let them know that you care about complying with the rules, which goes a long way when the final inspection comes around. Second, you save yourself time and money by setting things up the right way from the beginning without jeopardizing your opening with any last minute changes.

Health Pre-Inspection

For this pre-inspection contact your county or town's Health Department to send an inspector prior to construction. Similar to the fire marshall pre-inspection, this pre-inspection will benefit you in two very important ways. You show your concern and respect for what they require as well as create fewer chances for mistakes in your construction process.

So what do you need to ask the health inspector? If you need to build a bar at your venue make sure you tell the inspector where you are going to build the bar and let them know what the size and other specifics are going to be. The Health Department has a lot of rules and regulations about the bar and it's set up, so definitely have them tell you exactly what you need. The same goes for any building in the kitchen area as well.

The bathroom is a big hot spot area that the Health Department wants to ensure is up to code. Also, your inspector should explain lighting and water heater requirements as well as where they want the Fiberglass Reinforced Plastic (FRP) installed. FRP sheets are very expensive and tough to install, so you need to know exactly how much you need and where exactly you need to install it. If someone installs FRP in the wrong spot, it's a huge hassle (and big expensive) to add more!

Step 12: Design Bar Areas

Throughout the design process keep in mind how you want the bar to flow. The word "flow" refers to where you want customers and employees to move around the establishment. The flow of the bar must stay focused around efficiency, so staff members can shift throughout the crowds quickly and deliver drinks fast. Having the right flow maximizes sales, because the faster you can get a drink into a customer's hand the sooner they will drink and reorder. Slow drink delivery means bad service and ultimately less repeat business for you. Besides efficiency, the flow of your bar should also focus around having fun. When designing your bar layout, analyze whether customers can easily see and interact with each other customers as well as view entertainment without obstructions.

When a customer walks through the door of a bar they look for an attractive place to position themselves to socialize and relax. Obviously you'll have seating to accommodate the majority of customers, but pay attention to the areas away from the tables or bar as well. Get creative in your design and add some interesting spaces for customers to enjoy. For example, you could build a pony wall (a 4-6 feet high wall) with an attached drink rail and place barstool seating all the way down. Drink rails are great for crowded bars with standing room only, because customers can stand and socialize and still have a place to set their drinks down.

Creating Ambiance

When customers come into your bar they should be influenced to feel a certain way based on the mood or ambiance you create. You can have a different ambiance for day versus night and you can even create different moods for different sections of the bar, it's all up to you. For most of my bars I would have a more quiet, relaxed atmosphere during the day and a more lively and energetic atmosphere at night.

Different atmospheres to create include:

- Formal or informal
- Quiet or loud
- Cozy or spacious
- Modern or dated
- Romantic or social
- Leisurely or busy
- Comfortable or functional

4 Important (But Overlooked) Design Components

1) Flooring

Hopefully, the flooring in your lease space doesn't need to be entirely redone, but if it does you don't have to spend a fortune. Basically the front of the house (customer area) needs to be a material that's attractive and not slippery. Materials for flooring such as tile, wood, or waterproof concrete work really well here. The flooring in staff areas (kitchen and behind bar) should have a more functional role rather than decorative focus. Any material can work, but it's in your best interest to choose a material that's easy to clean with some sort of grit or texture on the surface to help improve staff footing. In the staff areas you should also add anti-fatigue mats and bar mats to provide extra cushion. These mats help your staff members stay comfortable during long shifts.

2) Ceiling

The ceiling is often overlooked, but should be considered in your design. If the ceiling looks presentable then by all means leave it alone and move on. If the ceiling needs some help then make the necessary repairs and then paint it a dark color. Try and stay away from a bright white color. Bars are normally geared around evening and night business, so I usually always go with black. Black also makes imperfections less visible, which is another great bonus.

3) Windows

Windows should be clean and in good shape for business. If the windows aren't tinted I suggest you speak with a few local tinting companies to get some quotes. Even if the sun doesn't glare through the windows during happy hour, tinting can help create a dimmer atmosphere for your evening crowd. Blinds or curtains can help as well, as long as they tie into your concept appropriately.

4) Lighting

With all of the interesting shapes, sizes, and colors available today, lighting is a key element in your bar's design. There's nothing more powerful in creating a mood than lighting (other than music, which we'll discuss more in *Step 16*). When you start designing each area of your bar take into consideration what you want in terms of lighting because you need to get lighting taken care of early in the construction process, so you aren't ripping walls apart late in the game.

If you have any steps or stairs inside or outside your bar, do your customers and staff members a big favor by providing adequate lighting around them. I add more direct lighting over stairs and sometimes even add rope lighting at the base of each stair so no one accidentally trips.

Different areas of your bar are required by law to have more light than others.

For example, in South Carolina the Health Department requires you to have certain lights throughout your establishment for cleanup. Once again, do your homework so you know what regulations you need to comply with.

When to Hire an Architect

If you have a significant amount of rebuilding to do, you may be required by the town or city to hire a professional architect. The architect does not have to be the best in town to get some good plans drawn up. I usually don't use architects, but on a few occasions I was forced by the city to use one. If I need an architect I will find them by other people's recommendations or I will shop around to find a good rate and professional service. I once received quotes from 2 different architects that ranged from $400 to $3,000 for the same project. I went with the $400 quote and received great drawings. If I hadn't shopped around, I would have gotten hosed for an extra $2,600. When you are just starting out, you can't take hits like this or you will run out of funds very quickly.

Key Areas to Focus Design Efforts on:

The 6 main bar areas include the bar, kitchen, entertainment area(s), bathrooms, office, and outside. The 7th area that I discuss is the entry way and it's only of importance for bars that serve large amounts of food. For each area I review the importance of the area, design strategy, flooring, and lighting. I also list important equipment and supply items, so you can start figuring out what you may or may not need and where things will go. Don't start ordering any bulky equipment and/or supply items until you know where you are going to put them and have the space measured to confirm the fit. In *Step 16* I discuss more equipment specifics as well as where to find equipment items.

Area 1: Bar

Importance:

The main bar area includes the staff area behind the bar, which consists of the back bar and under bar, as well as the customer area in front of the bar. The staff area needs to stay focused around function and efficiency, while the customer area needs to have a fun and appealing atmosphere. The bar area is your attention getter and moneymaker, so spend the majority of your energy and money in this area.

Design Strategy:

Obviously, if there's no pre-existing bar then you must build one. There are three main shapes of bars to consider: long and straight, horseshoe (semi-circle), or square shaped. Whichever style you choose to go with the 2 main design goals for your bar are staff efficiency and customer appeal. In my experience, square bars have always brought me in the most cash. I think square bars are the most functional and appealing of the 3 main bar shapes because the customers can all see and talk to one another easily and the staff can quickly see all of the customers at the bar and service them without having far to go. With the square bar, it's as if everyone's part of the party, which means people will stay longer and spend more money.

The height of the bar is important and standard bars usually measure 40-42 inches high. The width of the bar (between customer and bartender) should be between 24-36in. The length of the bar depends on how much space you have and how many people you would like to fit at the bar. In general, try and allow roughly 3 feet of personal space for each person at the bar.

Also make sure you add little touches like small hooks underneath the bar so ladies can hang their purses as well as a foot rail so people's legs aren't just dangling off the chairs.

If a bar already exists, see what you can salvage to save some money. The bar has to be nice, but it doesn't have to be brand new top of the line granite to make fantastic profits. Maybe you can add new countertops, refinish some wood paneling, or add an extension. Also check to see if the inside of the bar has an efficient set-up for staff members, because if it doesn't you will have to make a few changes.

The staff area of the bar is divided into 2 sections: the back bar and the under bar. The under bar is where the ice, beer, and glasses are kept.

The under bar needs to include the following elements:
- Inside of the bar should be covered in Fiberglass Reinforced Plastic (FRP) (Health Dept. pre-inspection hopefully helped give guidance here).
- Hot and cold water capability for sinks.
- Adequate space for alcohol, liquor, and food product storage, glass storage, and/or refrigeration.
- Raised floor drain under sinks.
- Extra power for the cooler, lights, and compressor.
- Space between bar and equipment for plumbing connections (Consult plumber on how much space is needed).
- Phone jack

The back bar is where liquor is kept and poured for the customer and is normally the background the customer sees when sitting at the bar. Take the customer's view in mind here and add some cool lighting around the bottles or some other unique design. Install some TV's, add some unique shelving for your liquor bottles, create a unique mural with your bar's name, and/or hang some promotional banners in your back bar.

Flooring:

Behind the bar you should have waterproof concrete or quarry tile with some kind of grit so staff won't slip (Anti-slip / Anti-fatigue mats are great). Flooring in the customer area of the bar should be designed to be attractive and safe, so even a simple tile works great here.

Lighting Issues:

Incorporate decorative lighting into your bar design to draw some extra attention to your bar. Lighting should always be dimmed a little in the evening and night hours, so make sure you have dimming capabilities built in. If lighting is too bright, customers will feel like they are in a spotlight and if it's too dark they won't be able to see. You must find a comfortable middle ground.

Some states have regulations about lighting behind the bar, so check with your state's health department to see what they require. In South Carolina you need to have a strip of lighting over the sinks (placed under the bar). The Health Department also has rules on the type of lighting needed in the bar area for after hours cleanup, so find out what specific lighting they want installed.

Some areas behind the bar like the ice well, might be hard to see when you dim the lights for night business. I've used rope lighting in the past, which is very inexpensive and provides just the right amount of light for dark areas.

Equipment:

- 3 Bay Sink (see *Step 16*)
- Blender(s), juicer, frozen beverage dispenser
- TV(s) (see *Step 16* for more information)
- Service well (see *Step 16*)
- Soda guns (see *Step 16*)
- Draft beer station
- Glass washer
- Small refrigerators (for added beer and wine storage)
- Cutting board
- Spill Mats
- Speed rails
- Towel Holders
- Bin for dirty towels
- Tables and Seating (see *Step 16*)
- POS System (see *Step 16*)
- Beer and wine bottle openers, can openers
- Different glasses (i.e. shot, wine, beer, liquor, martini, margarita)
- Silverware

- Bar mixing book with drink recipes
- Ice scoops, tongs, bar spoons
- Measured liquor pour spouts
- Cocktail shakers
- First aid kit
- Fire extinguisher
- Trash can
- Portable yellow caution signs for wet floors
- Phone
- Speakers (*see Step 16*)

Supplies:

- Menus
- Napkins, coasters, placemats
- Straws, stirrers, toothpicks
- Cleaning supplies, towels, dish rags, rubber gloves
- Matches, cigarettes to sell (check local/state regulations), ashtrays (if smoking is allowed buy 1 ashtray for every 2 seats in your establishment and buy the cheap ones because they disappear)
- Pens, paper
- Emergency numbers posted (Fire and Police Department)

Pro Tip: To go along with the main bar I suggest adding a creative secondary bar to really make your establishment unique. A secondary bar could be a smaller satellite bar away from the main bar or a small segment of the main bar. Either one you choose, the secondary bar can add more appeal and more profits. Some secondary bars to consider in your design include a shot bar, daiquiri bar, margarita bar, beer garden, martini bar, and/or sangria bar.

Area 2: Kitchen

Importance:

This area must be designed around creating a quality product. The kitchen can be a very hectic area for your staff, so organization is a must to increase staff efficiency. Your kitchen does not have to be very big or decked out with fancy equipment to produce some appealing food choices as long as you stay creative with your menu. Regardless of the kitchen size, you should serve food of some sort. Customers stay longer and spend more money when they don't have to leave your bar to find food.

Design Strategy:
The following items should be incorporated into your design:
- Fiberglass Reinforced Plastic (FRP) placed on walls around cooking area for easier cleanup (required by Health Department)
- Floor drain (for ice machine)
- Proper plumbing, electrical wiring, and gas lines put in (please consult experts here)
- Area(s) for storage of food products (used and unused) as well as cooking equipment, utensils.
- Work surfaces that will come in contact with food kept separate from work surfaces not in contact with food.
- Mop area with floor drain

Even if you don't plan on serving much food you still have to follow all state regulations for the kitchen area, so find out what your specific state requires.

Flooring:

Flooring in the kitchen needs to be safe and comfortable for staff members (especially for cooks that are standing for long shifts). Make sure you have a floor with some sort of grit and add anti-slip/anti-fatigue floor mats around the prep/cook stations.

Lighting Issues:

Lighting should be bright throughout the kitchen for the obvious reasons that staff must ensure proper food preparation and cleanly work areas. The Health Department has specific codes regarding the lighting in the kitchen….check them!

Equipment:

You don't want to spend a lot of money on kitchen equipment if your main goal is to serve alcohol. You can always upgrade equipment or add more equipment after you start bringing in revenue. The key now is to only choose the equipment you need to prepare your opening menu. If you plan to offer some simple bar food then don't waste your money on a full-scale commercial range with hood and ansul system, when all you need is maybe only a fryer, microwave, and pizza oven. You also don't want to have so much equipment that it's impossible to find things and move easily around the kitchen. Spend some time measuring the space to figure out what equipment fits as well as thinking about what menu items you want to serve. Also don't forget to check state regulations to see what kitchen equipment they require you to have.

Some common equipment you might consider include:
- 3 bay sink (see *Step 16* for more information)
- Hand sink for staff (see *Step 16* for more information)

- Hood and Ansul system
- Grease trap (If you are serving food the Health department will require you to have a certain size. Large ones can be placed outside, while smaller ones can be attached to a counter).
- Oven (gas or convection), stove (great for small kitchens)
- Grill
- Fryers, microwave, sandwich press, toaster, counter top oven, pizza oven (all of these items are great for small kitchens with limited space)
- Food scale
- Hot and cold prep tables
- Refrigerators, Freezers
- Food warmers
- Dishwasher
- Dish racks
- Food processor
- Ice machine
- Coffee maker, tea press
- Storage containers
- Carts/shelving
- Garbage can
- Pots, pans
- Mixing bowls, spatulas
- Set of knives
- Serving trays
- Dishes
- Silverware
- Thermometer
- Fire extinguisher

Supplies:

- Paper towels, napkins
- Styrofoam containers (for take out)
- Plastic silverware (for take out)
- Cleaning supplies (mops, soap, bleach)
- Measuring Supplies
- Tin foil, saran wrap, plastic bags
- Rubber gloves
- Hair nets

Pro Tip: I avoid purchasing most of the costly kitchen equipment in this section by offering a limited, yet creative menu at most of my bars. You only need the equipment necessary to create the menu items you plan to serve, so I recommend you plan your menu accordingly.

Area 3: Bar Entertainment Area(s)

Importance:

Maximize your customers experience and increase profits with additional entertainment.

Design Strategy:

Incorporate one or more of these different types of entertainment areas into your design:
- Lounge (sofa seating with low tables)
- Indoor/Outdoor game area (electronic gambling games, billiards, darts, or corn hole)
- Dance floor (wood flooring, DJ booth)
- VIP area (Raised floor with seating for groups/private parties)

Flooring:

Depends on your design, but keep it attractive and definitely not slippery.

Lighting Issues:

Use the lighting to enhance whatever mood you are trying to create in this area. Remember you may still need certain lights installed for after-hours cleanup.

Equipment:

- TV(s) (*see Step 16*)
- Speakers (*see Step 16*)
- Tables/seating
- Games: darts, pool table, electronic video games

Supplies: Depends on your design!

Pro Tip: Some states allow private businesses to have Electronic

Gambling Devices (EGDs) such as standalone slot machines, video poker, video keno, etc. If your state allows you to have one, I strongly recommend you place one in your bar and encourage your customers to play. Of course there are winners and you must pay out from time to time, but over the long run you are the big winner.

Area 4: Bathrooms

Importance:

People unconsciously base a portion of the overall bar experience on the state of the bathroom. Not surprisingly, women place a higher importance on the state of the bathroom than men.

Design Strategy:

Even though it's the bathroom try not to ignore this area. Keep the design simple while tying in little touches of your main theme. This area has to adhere to certain health codes, but hopefully you chose a lease where the bathroom is already up to code so you can save big money.

Men's and women's bathrooms each have certain needs you should cater to. I always place more emphasis on making the women's bathroom nice by adding larger mirrors and warmer lighting.

Flooring:

Non-Slip tile works great for easy cleanup.

Lighting Issues:

Use warm lighting or dimmer lighting in bathrooms (especially in the women's).

Equipment:

Your equipment needs are slightly different for the women's and men's bathrooms. I recommend that for both bathrooms you consider placing promotional advertisements in the bathroom stalls and/or in a display case as you walk in. When customers are standing in line or doing you know what, it's a great opportunity to grab their attention about an upcoming event.

For women's bathrooms:
- Multiple toilets and sinks are a plus
- Stall dividers with doors

- Drink rail to set drinks on
- Purse hooks in stalls and by sinks
- Trash cans in each stall and by sinks
- Paper towel dispenser
- Toilet paper dispensers that hold large quantities of paper

For men's bathrooms:
- Multiple urinals are a plus with at least one toilet stall with door
- Sinks
- Drink holders
- Trash cans by the sinks
- Tile on the walls (for some reason men like to punch walls in bar bathrooms, so this prevents that from happening)
- Urinal dividers
- Paper towel dispenser
- Toilet paper dispenser in stalls

Supplies:

- Toilet paper
- Paper towels
- Soap
- A nice smelling hand scrub or lotion is a nice touch for women's bathroom.

Area 5: Office

Importance:

You need a space where paper work and other administrative work can be completed without having to leave the bar. You can also use this area for protected liquor storage.

Design Strategy:

The bottom line when constructing your office is to make sure it's a nice, organized work environment, if not then you (or your manager) will spend less time completing the necessary paperwork and your business will suffer.

Make sure to incorporate:
- Outlets for computer/printer
- Phone jack
- Dead bolt lock on the door
- Shelving for liquor storage

Flooring and Lighting Issues:

This is a workspace for management only, so do as you wish.

Equipment:

- Desk and Chair(s)
- Securable safe to store smaller change for registers (ex: rolls of coins, $1, $5, and $10 bills)
- Filing cabinets with locks
- Phone
- Computer (never allow staff members to use the computer for personal use)
- TV (sometimes its nice to take a little break away from customers and staff)
- All in One Printer (printer/copier/fax)
- Camera Monitor (its nice to monitor business while getting paperwork done at the same time). Look to *Step 14* for more information on choosing cameras.

Supplies:

- Calculator
- Paper
- Back up ink cartridges (never throw away old ink cartridges, take them to Staples to receive store credit)
- Filing folders
- Pens (Servers always lose these, so if this becomes a problem start charging $1 per pen. I guarantee they will start bringing their own.)

An organized and clean office can save you hours of work. One of my biggest mistakes starting out in this business was my inability to stay organized. I would waste countless hours trying to find documents or receipts I needed. This happened over and over until I finally got fed up and made it a point of not leaving work until everything was cleaned and put back into place.

Area 6: Outside

Importance:

The exterior of your establishment should have great curb appeal to attract customers all on it's own. You want customers to have positive thoughts about your bar before they even walk through the door. Also, if your city has a ban on indoor smoking, your customers who smoke will greatly appreciate even the smallest outdoor seating area.

63

Design Strategy:

Additional space outside should be used for extra seating and customer enjoyment. Even a sidewalk can fit a few high top tables and chairs. As long as the weather is nice, people love to enjoy the outdoors. Just make sure that you get permission from the landlord and/or obtain any necessary permits from the city before you add anything to the outside.

Some exterior improvements to consider include:
- Painting the exterior building and/or door
- Constructing an overhang or awning
- Constructing a porch, deck, or patio
- Constructing a small bar

Lighting:

Parking lot lighting: Must have adequate lighting in the parking lot area for customer safety and comfort.
Exterior lighting: Bar needs adequate lighting on the front so people passing can easily locate your bar. Have extra lighting placed on your signage as well.
Outdoor Patio/Seating: Make sure customers can see their drinks and food. Special outdoor lighting or even tiki torches can do the trick.

Equipment:

- Weather proof tables and seating (if possible)
- A small satellite bar or beer tub (possibly portable)
- Garbage can(s)
- Cigarette disposal bin and/or ashtrays
- TV's
- Speakers
- Awning
- Heaters (depends on your location)
- Broom(s)
- Shovels for walkways (if snow is an issue)

Supplies:

- Depends what you have going on outside!

Pro Tip: At the end of each day send a staff member out to pick up trash from around the parking lot. It won't take a lot of time or effort (hopefully), but it will help improve customers' first impressions and your relationship with your landlord.

Area 7: Entry Way (only important if you serve meals at your establishment)

Importance:

You want all customers greeted well and given a great first impression. If you serve meals at your establishment then have a host or hostess welcome everyone warmly and seat each party. This method will help you get customers seated quickly instead of hanging out in the entryway where they might make the decision to turn around and walk out. If you aren't serving much food or have a limited menu then you can allow customers to seat themselves.

Construction Strategy: (only if you are serving meals)

No construction necessary here. Our main goal here is to create a slight barrier from the rest of the establishment.

Equipment:

- Hostess Stand
- 2 Mats (1 placed on either side of door)

Supplies:

- Menus

Step 13: Create Logo and Order Signage

Your logo appears on all of your advertising and marketing material, so what kind of image do you want to portray? You don't need anything very complicated just think of McDonald's golden arches or Wendy's redheaded girl with pigtails. Simplicity is often better because it's always easier to remember.

Whatever your ideas are, hire a graphic design artist to get the job done. For professional logos done at competitive pricing, I recommend going online and using Elance. With Elance you can post your project and have graphic design artists from all around the World bid on your project. I have had logos designed through Elance for as little as $50.

Pro Tip: Before you spend money on having your logo and signage created, do a double check with a lawyer to make sure your bar's name isn't already trademarked. You don't need anyone coming after you pursuing damages. Also, think about having your own bar's name trademarked. Personally I have never trademarked the name of one of my bars, but that's because I always knew I would sell the bar as soon as it was profitable so I took the risk of someone copying my name. If you are planning to hold your business for years to come and/or expand to another location then getting a trademark now is a great idea. The trademark will protect you and give you exclusive rights to your name.

Order Signage

Every city has different rules and regulations about putting signs up. Some cities require signage to be within a certain size or only certain materials. For example, some cities do not allow neon signs. Even if your city allows a certain type of sign, still pursue approval from your landlord as well. You don't need to spend money on a sign only to find out that you need to take it down. Most cities require you to obtain permits for any signage you want to display. Luckily, for a few extra dollars many sign companies will submit all of the paperwork for you. I have found that it's well worth having a sign company take care of everything for you.

Whatever you do make sure your signs are as visible as possible. Bigger signs are always better and if you are allowed to have the kind that illuminate at night, go for it. You want to draw attention to your bar, so it's hard for people to miss. Potential customers should be able to see your sign from far away, so if your bar is set in a plaza or hidden off a side road try and place a sign close to the nearest road.

ONLINE RESOURCES:

1) Create a Logo:
http://www.elance.com
Elance is great for a variety of projects for your bar, but I'm bringing it up here specifically for the purpose of hiring a graphic designer to create a logo for your bar. Setting up an account with Elance and posting projects for experts to bid on is absolutely free. Only experts that meet your specifications will be allowed to bid on your project and you can view their bid, their past work, as well as client feedback. You are never obligated to hire anyone, so go take a look.

Phase 2: Pre-Construction Summary
Complete Steps Simultaneously

Step 10: Obtain Permits, Licenses, and Insurance
- Find out what permits/license you need to open and operate your bar.
- Business license, liquor license, and building permit are 3 of the most common permits/licenses you will need.
- Contact local and state organizations to gain more information about the regulations you need to follow in your operation.
- Talking to other local bar owners can help you gain insight into the challenges of opening.
- Speak with 3 different local insurance companies to get quotes on policies.
- Make sure you understand the terms of your insurance policy.

Step 11: Schedule Pre-Inspections
- Pre-Inspections save smart bar owners (like you) time and money and show the inspector that you care about adhering to their rules.
- 2 pre-Inspections you should schedule: Fire and Health Department pre-Inspection.

Step 12: Design Bar Areas
- The "flow" of your bar should be centered around staff efficiency and customer appeal/entertainment.
- If you have a lot of construction planned, hire an architect.
- The flooring, ceiling, windows, and lighting are design components that are too important to overlook.
- Design all areas of the bar including the 6 most important: bar, kitchen, entertainment areas, bathrooms, office, outside.
- Don't forget that each area of your bar has a different design strategy as well as different equipment and supply needs.

Step 13: Create Logo and Order Signage
- You need to have a logo created for your signs and marketing materials.
- Local graphic design artists are usually more expensive than hiring someone through an online company such as Elance.
- Hire a local sign company to create your signage and see if they can help you obtain the necessary permits (if applicable).
- Local graphic design artists are usually more expensive than hiring someone through an online company such as Elance.
- Hire a local sign company to create your signage and see if they can help you obtain the necessary permits (if applicable).

Phase 3: Construction

Attack Steps in Order

Step 14: Set-up Cameras & Alarm System

Before you start the actual construction, contact the local water and electric companies. Plan to have your utilities turned on when you are actually present, in order to monitor any issues that might come up. Past tenants sometimes leave faucets on or rip things out of the wall that could potentially cause flooding once the water is turned back on.

Surveillance Camera Set-Up

Every bar owner should have surveillance cameras up and running before bringing in expensive construction materials and equipment. I had a friend, who a few years ago owned a bar down the street from mine and before he could open the doors to the public somebody broke in and stole $20k worth of TVs. He didn't have an alarm system or any surveillance cameras up and running yet, so the robbers got away scotch free. $20k is a hard loss to bounce back from, especially before you are even open for business. Unfortunately people can't be trusted and you have to protect yourself early in the game. You shouldn't risk a large chunk of your investment if you don't have to.

Choosing Cameras

First, find some video cameras with networking capability. The best systems out there in my opinion are Cisco Systems cameras. Camera systems like Cisco's have web login capabilities that allow monitoring of your bar from remote locations as long as you have online access.

The office in your bar should have a monitor that has live streaming camera footage available for viewing at all times. Having this system will help you and/or a manager keep an eye on things, while getting other work done at the same time.

Pro Tip: Your staff should know that you are always checking up on them. If you see behavior caught on camera that you don't like then confront them. This way you can keep them on their toes and help improve their performance. Remember though, the cameras shouldn't by any means replace an on site manager.

Camera Positioning

The camera company helps determine how many cameras you need. Personally I like to cover every area of my bar with cameras, but that's just me. I've seen some crazy things happen in this business and I feel more comfortable having footage of every angle so I can monitor staff. Not all of my bars had cameras and that was a huge mistake. Without cameras it's easier for staff members to steal inventory and slack on responsibilities.

The camera company should also help you decide where to place your cameras. No matter what, you need to have the following areas covered: front door, back door, cash register, and the area around your safe in the office. When positioning the camera around the safe, make sure the camera is positioned to catch a perfect view of a person's face should they choose to mess with your safe.

Choose an Alarm System

When looking for an alarm system, choose one that interfaces easily with the surveillance cameras. Go ahead and get quotes from three different companies (you should know my 3 quote rule by now). Make sure you negotiate your quotes, because they are usually allowed to come down on price as well as throw in some extra perks. I always get them to the point where they have to talk to their manager and ask for permission for something. This usually lets me know that they are close to giving the best rate possible.

The security company will ask you to set up codes to enable and disable the system. Set up a master code for you as well as sub codes for a manager or anyone else you want to have open or close the bar. If an incident happens you can go back and look at the last code used to figure out who was responsible. Another bonus feature is that you may check the time when the alarm was enabled or disabled, which proves extremely useful when you suspect your staff of closing early or staying too late to party.

The security company also asks for a contact if the system is activated and that person should be you or an on-call manager. Expect to get a call at least once or twice a year, especially if your alarm system is motion activated. The motion sensors are very sensitive and even a bug moving across the sensor could trigger the alarm.

Pro Tip: Unless you enjoy getting out of bed at 4am, I suggest that you secure and fasten everything in the bar so not even a breeze from the air conditioning could budge it. I once made the mistake of leaving balloons up after a party and I didn't even make it into my driveway before I got a call from the alarm company telling me the alarm had been triggered. Going back to your bar after a long day and night is not fun, believe me.

ONLINE RESOURCES:

1) Find a Surveillance System:
http://www.Ciscosystems.com
I have used Cisco systems in the past and definitely recommend their security services, but that shouldn't deter you from getting quotes from a few other companies as well.

Step 15: Manage Construction

Constructing a bar usually requires hiring the following 5 specialists. Depending on your bar design, you may need to hire more or less workers.

1) Plumber
- Install extra sinks (kitchen/bathrooms/bar area)
- Install ice machine(s)

2) Electrician
- Camera Set-Up
- Wiring for lighting inside/outside
- Installing phone jacks and outlets if needed
- Wiring for equipment setup
- Runs more power behind bar if needed (coolers usually need more power to run)

3) Building Contractor
- Flooring, walls
- Any major construction (pony walls, booths, bar)

4) Painter
- Handles ceiling and wall issues
- Paints (obviously)

I always hire cheap helpers to paint, such as friends or local teenagers. Professional painters can be very expensive, so if you have major ceiling or wall issues have your building contractor fix them first then start painting. It's not worth paying the money for a painting specialist in my book, unless you need some special mural or design done.

5) Audio Specialist
- Speaker and sound system installation

Choosing Workers
Get three different quotes for each type of specialist you need to hire. Look for professional behavior as well as good rates, because you need the job completed correctly in a timely manner. If they are slow getting back to you with a quote or seem unprofessional then they probably aren't someone you want to do business with regardless of their fees.

Another option is to hire a company that puts everything together for you, however, this is extremely costly and won't necessarily save you time.

Pro Tip: Sometimes you can pay construction or maintenance workers with a bar tab instead of cash. Not everyone goes for this, but many workers are happy to accept. I always try to entice workers to accept a bar tab as pay because a $100 bar tab might only cost me around $40, so I always save money when paying with bar tabs.

Managing Construction

If you want the project to run smoothly you must schedule the workers accordingly. Many times the specialists need to work together on projects. For example the plumber will do some work and then have to wait on the contractor to come in and build something before they can finish the plumbing job. You need to get everyone on the same page early or you will only waste your time and money. Your lease payment, water and electric bills won't stop coming because you aren't open to the public, so get going!

ONLINE RESOURCES:

Hire specialists to get your bar up and running:

http://www.Bidclerk.com, **1-877-737-6482**
Submit a commercial project posting directly through this web site free of charge. After the project is submitted, someone from the reporting staff contacts you to verify the details of the project and uploads plans if you have them available. Contractors in your area then bid on your project. The following address is a direct link to submit a project:http://www.bidclerk.com/projects/submitProject1.jsp

http://www.servicemagic.com/commercial/, **1-877-947-3639**
ServiceMagic Business connects business owners with pre-screened, top-rated service professionals. This is another great site that allows you to post jobs for contractors to bid on for free.

http://www.angieslist.com, **1-888-888-LIST**
Angie's List gives access to customer reviews of local service providers. This is great when you are deciding whom to hire for your construction projects. One cool part about Angie's List is that customers rate the service providers and the service providers are allowed to respond. If the provider gets a justifiable bad score and never responds they are put in Angie's "penalty box," which means their name will appear in the Angie's List magazine for 3 consecutive months and on their website indefinitely. Any provider that is serious about business will try and make the situation right, so they aren't bad mouthed. I like this idea because it holds contractors more accountable than usual. To use Angie's List you have to become a member and your rates will vary depend on how developed the actual "list" of contractors is in your area.

Step 16: Find Equipment, Supplies, and Services

Go back to *Step 12* to see what equipment and supplies you will need for each area of your bar. As you can imagine it's extremely easy to get carried away with spending, so a great way to stay on budget is to look for used equipment and supplies. Check in the local newspapers from surrounding towns as well as Craigslist for any equipment you could possibly use. Fortunately for you and me, lots of restaurants fail so there are lots of people out there stuck with leftovers. Most people are desperate to get just about anything back for the equipment, so this is the perfect opportunity for you to save some big money. I normally buy used restaurant equipment for 10 to 30 cents on the dollar. The downside to buying used equipment is that you won't get any warranties like you would if you were buying new equipment, but that's never been an issue for me. I always buy as much used equipment as I can and I haven't had a problem yet (knock on wood).

Leasing Equipment/Supplies

Some equipment can still be tough to afford even if it's used, so leasing is sometimes a better option. By leasing equipment you can get in the game faster without having to fork over thousands of dollars. In the long run it's cheaper to own the equipment, but at least you can take your time and wait to buy equipment after you start bringing money in. See the ONLINE RESOURCES at the end of this section for equipment companies that offer leasing.

Items to lease:
- Kitchen and bar equipment (ovens, stoves, ansul system, ice machines, coolers, portable bars)
- POS system
- Towels/linens/doormats- some companies provide clean replacements for these items on a weekly basis. These companies make money by billing the restaurants and bars for the weekly laundry services.

Free Equipment (well, almost)

When you buy the inventory and supplies you need, some companies provide the necessary equipment that goes along with it. For example, when I buy coffee and tea from a certain company they automatically provide me with coffee makers, tea presses, and filters at no extra charge (as long as I keep buying their products). The company I buy paper towels and toilet paper from also install the plastic holders in the bathrooms and kitchen at no extra cost. Also, the company that sells me soda installs soda guns and all of the lines that run to the CO_2 tank at no extra cost. All of these examples should show you why you need to ask what each supplier can provide you with. Don't miss out on the extras!

Dealing with Suppliers/Vendors

There are so many different types of suppliers out there and they all offer different products. Some companies provide a vast array of products while some specialize in only a few specific items. Once you find as much affordable equipment as possible, make a list of all the remaining equipment and supplies you still need. Chances are the suppliers in the area already found your bar and have contacted you, so you should have their contact information available. Call or e-mail them to find out which vendors carry the items on your list as well as their rates.

Pro Tip: The suppliers are out to take advantage of you by making you pay top dollar, so you must use the different companies against each other to get the best quotes. One might charge you $3,000 more for an item than another vendor, so negotiate with them until you get one of the companies down to the best price for each item. I will sometimes even hand quotes from one company over to show the other, in order to get them to come down on price. There's nothing wrong\g with some healthy competition, right?

Bypass Vendors

These days you can save yourself the time and hassle of dealing with pushy vendors and go directly online to find the equipment you need with leasing options as well. The best part is that you can do it in the privacy of your own office and have everything delivered straight to your door. Please see the ONLINE RESOURCES at the end of this section for sites to visit.

Important Equipment Items that Every Bar Needs

1) Sound System/Theater System
Its important to have a sound system, but don't worry about having a top of the line system to get started. Once you start making cash, you can always upgrade at a later date. Definitely check in the newspaper and Craigslist for a used system. I once found a $3,000 system for $150, because some guy went out of the club business and was storing the system in his garage and his wife wanted it out. I can't tell you how happy I was that day. Deals that good are tough to find, but they are out there.

I'm a big fan of Sam's club for sound systems, because you can get a good sound system for around $300. Why spend thousands when you only need a few hundred? Believe me, the $300 system gives more than enough sound to blow your customers out of their seats (not that you really want to do that, but you get my point).

Depending on what music you want to play at your bar you should consider an MP3 player for downloaded music, or satellite radio. It's up to you. Personally, I use both. Whatever you, stay away from CD players. CD players are outdated and your bartender might not always remember to change the CDs and then your customers will get sick of your music and leave.

Speaker Set-Up
Instead of figuring this out on your own, have an audio specialist do this for you. Some audio specialists try and make you buy things from them, but stick with a moderate speaker system of your choice (doesn't have to be top of the line) and have them place speakers where they deem appropriate. Speaker placement can be tricky because you don't want speakers too close to the bar that people have to yell when making conversation, but at the same time you want it to seem like sound is coming from everywhere. Just let the professionals handle this.

2) TVs
In this day and age you absolutely need to have TVs at your bar. Always go with flat screens and make sure you have at least one positioned at the main bar.
The best place to find a deal on a TV is Sam's Club or Costco. Buy them new or even check the ones that have been returned back to the store and are offered for 30-50% less. A lot of people don't look at these discounted TVs because the boxes are gone. Most of the time there is nothing wrong with them, it's only company policy that returned TVs must be sold again without a box. Don't let that deter you from saving big money.

3) Tables and Seating
A great bar has attractive and comfortable seating. The seats need to have a back on them or at the very least be padded and comfortable to allow for many hours of relaxed seating. The more comfortable your customers are, the happier they will be, and the longer they will stay in your establishment. Make sure your seating matches up to the height of the tables or bar you have. Instead of guessing the height get out the measuring tape to figure out exactly what you need. Some different types of tables and seating to consider in the different areas of your bar are booths, bar stools, banquette seating, modular seating, and couches.

4) POS System
These can cost a lot of money up front, but in the long run you will save yourself money by preventing theft. You will also save yourself from countless hours of manually generating reports. POS systems come with cash registers and track everything for you, and I mean everything. I think the Aloha models are the best in the business and the easiest to use. With the touch of a button, you can track the daily, weekly, monthly sales of every single item you serve. You can also run a report on server's sales and performance and keep track of your inventory usage.

Many different sales companies sell Aloha models, so make sure you get quotes from a few companies. Since POS systems are an expensive investment (they can go for around $10k) explore a lease option to make it more affordable.

Pro Tip: Whatever you do, please don't use a hand written ticket system. I've tried the ticket system before in an effort to save money and it turned into a huge disaster. A ticket system will set you up for theft all day, everyday from your staff. Don't even tempt staff members, because you have plenty of other things to worry about. I hope you make the right decision and listen to my years of experience!

5) CO2 Tank & Soda Guns

CO_2 provides the pressure you need to power your soda guns and kegs. Normally, as soon as I have the bar built I have the soda guns and CO_2 installed. If you check your phone book or do a search on the internet you should find a company or two that will provide you tanks to lease. You can buy a small tank, but I've found it's just as cheap to lease a bigger one. Bigger tanks are normally kept outside behind your bar, while smaller tanks can fit in the kitchen or in a corner of your bar. I personally like leasing bigger tanks and keeping them outside, because the CO_2 company checks them regularly and handles refills without me having to call them. Anything automatic saves me valuable time to do other things.

Your soda company provider (Coke, Pepsi, or generic company) will install your soda guns and install the lines from the CO_2 tank. They will either run the lines up the ceiling or install them in the wall and all you have to do is pay for the soda.

6) Ice Machine

In my eyes, ice machines are the lifeblood of the bar business. Without ice you can't serve cold beers or cocktails, so what good would you be to customers? Well, you probably wouldn't have customers. That being said I recommend starting off with a smaller ice machine and then wait to see what kind of volume you are going to do first. Ice machines are made based on how many pounds of ice they can hold at one time. I wouldn't go smaller than a 650 lb. capacity machine, but I wouldn't go to the extreme end either and buy one that has a 2000 lb. capacity and costs thousands of dollars if my volume doesn't support it. A 650-800 lb. ice machine should be all you need (unless your place is bigger than 5,000 sq. ft.). If your find that your business needs more ice, you can always upgrade or buy another ice machine down the road.

I always try and find used ice machines to save some money, but if you are worried about it breaking down you can always buy one new or lease a new one. Ice machines are expensive to buy and maintain, but they are cheaper than buying bags of ice everyday.

Certain ice machines produce different shapes of ice. The 3 main shapes of ice are cubes, flakes, and nuggets. I have used both cubed ice machines and nugget ice machines. Cube ice machines produce a harder square ice cube that melts slowly, while the nuggets produce a softer chewable ice. The flake producing ice machines aren't as useful in the bar business, because you can always just use a blender to produce smaller pieces of ice if you need. I think the cube ice machines are your best bet for quality drinks, but nugget ice machines are fine if you have a more laid back bar such as a pub, tavern, sports bar, or college bar. If you have an upscale concept I would choose the cubed ice machine. The cubed ice machines come in 2 variations: whole dice and half-dice sized ice. I prefer the smaller sized cubes because you can fit more ice into glasses, creating great looking drinks.

In regards to cooling systems, air-cooled machines are easier to install and cost less to purchase and operate than water-cooled machines. I recommend looking into the Manitowoc or Scotsman brands of ice machines.

You must get professional help when installing your ice machine. Electrical and water connections as well as a floor drain must be within 6 feet of the ice machine. Have a plumber make sure the ice machine is connected to a cold water supply and have separate drain lines for the machine and the bin. Also, all machines are offered in a variety of voltages, so make sure the one you choose meets your requirements.

The placement of the ice machine is important because your servers and bartenders need easy accessibility to chill down beers or serve cold drinks. Remember the faster you can get a drink in a customers hand, the more money you make. I usually keep an ice machine in the kitchen and constantly have staff members fill buckets and transport ice into the ice wells. I usually use a 5 gallon bucket and label it "Ice Only," so no one uses it to clean the bathroom or anything else that could jeopardize the health of my customers.

7) Service Well
The service well holds the ice behind the bar so it's easily accessible to bartenders and servers to ice down cold beer and drinks. Depending on the size of your bar you may have one or two service wells or even more. Try to situate the service well towards the end of the bar, so waitresses won't interfere with bartenders business.

You must make sure bartenders use the ice scoop to get the ice out of the service well and into your cup for drinks. What you don't want (and it happens all the time) is for bartenders to rush and take a glass and put it straight into the service well to get ice. This is a big mistake, because the glass can break. Plastic cups are fine, but the ones made out of glass don't always make it. Now if the glass breaks in your ice well you are left with a big dilemma. Your staff better learn quickly to immediately pour cranberry juice or tomato juice all over the ice well so other staff members know that the ice well needs cleaned out. The last thing you need is for a staff member to serve pieces of the ice and broken glass to your customers. Talk about a lawsuit waiting to happen.

8) Sinks
3 Bay Sink: So what's a 3 bay sink? A 3 bay sink has 3 compartments used for

washing, rinsing, and sanitizing. The sink is a bar and restaurant industry standard and is usually required by the health department along with 2 drain boards (usually welded to the sink). When purchasing a sink, check that it's NSF (National Sanitation Foundation) approved. If you serve food at your bar you must have a 3 bay sink in your kitchen as well as behind the bar.

Employee Sinks: The Health Department requires you to have separate hand sinks for employee use in food preparation or cooking areas.

Important Services That Every Bar Needs

Let's go over some weekly and monthly services you must consider for your bar.

1) Trash Removal / Grease pickup
Go ahead and get quotes from 3 different garbage companies. You've got to get a dumpster on the premises for all the trash and bottles you go through everyday.

Grease is not something you want to throw away in the trash. I've always had someone approach me about picking up my grease for free. I even had a guy that paid me money every week to pick up my grease! It wasn't very much, but I didn't mind taking it! Some companies recycle the grease to make fuel, so you might be able to get some extra money for something you need to dispose of anyway.

2) Payroll
I've done payroll on my own before and it's too easy to make mistakes. Since then I always outsource payroll and pay on a semi-monthly schedule, because it's less expensive than bi-weekly. There are 24 semi-monthly payrolls in a year, while there are 26 payrolls a year for bi-weekly. Basically you save money on 2 payrolls with the semi-monthly payroll.

3) Accounting
I always use an accountant for my taxes. Even if you normally do your own taxes I recommend hiring a professional to prepare your local, state, and federal tax returns for your new business. Having the accountant complete taxes as well as go over your profits and losses is well worth the extra money.

4) Cleaning (bar and linens)
I usually have my staff members clean after shifts, but I know of other bar owners who bring in an outside cleaning company to do a thorough cleaning. I personally prefer saving the money.
You also need cleaning for your linens, towels, doormats, and aprons. Some companies provide all of the linen items you need and then give you fresh supplies each week, while only charging for the cost of laundry. I prefer going this route instead of buying all the linens on my own and washing them.

5) Internet / Telephone

6) Electric / Gas / Water

7) Satellite TV / Cable

Basically, if your bar only has one TV then you can get by with simple cable TV. I only recommend going with cable if you are opening a small wine, martini, piano, or tapas bar, where the focus is not around watching sporting events. That's not to say that if you open a bar with one of these themes you can't have multiple TVs and satellite, I'm just saying that you can get away with cable more often than other bar themes.

8) Merchant Services

A merchant account gives you the capability to process credit cards as payment with your POS system. If you choose not to have a POS system then you need a merchant terminal included with your merchant services account, however, I don't recommend going this route. POS systems are an absolute MUST in my opinion.

Work on obtaining three quotes from three different merchant companies. Fees and transaction costs vary greatly between companies, as well as the level of customer service they provide. If the system goes down on a busy night (and it will) you need a provider to have a 24-hour customer support line to get your system up and running again. The name of the game is to save as much money as possible and have the least amount of problems, so spend some time picking the right company for the job.

Personally, I like to set up merchant accounts with my local bank because that's where my money is going anyway. I take the quotes from other companies and then present them to my bank to get them to come down on their fees, because they are usually on the high end.

Pro Tip: Beware of merchant account scams with non-bank companies. I have a friend who set up a merchant account for one of his bars and after accruing about $10,000 worth of sales in his terminal, he found out that he was never going to get his money because the company was in trouble and went out of business. The main problem was that the company was outside of the United States, so it was nearly impossible to pursue legal action to recover the loss.

9) Music

Certain satellite TV companies sell packages that include XM stations, so if you pay for one of these packages you can kill two birds with one stone and purchase your television and music together.

I can't stress to you enough what an important role music plays in the bar business.

You must always have music playing in the background to appeal to the kind of customer you want to attract. I normally tailor my music choices to the time of day. Through lunch, dinner, and happy hour I usually play soft rock for a bar that's more laid back and for a more upscale bar I will play mellow lounge music. For a late night crowd I always go with more upbeat and modern music.

Pro Tip: Over the years I have witnessed firsthand how music sets the mood in a bar. A fellow bar owner once told me that when a rowdy crowd looks like they might start a fight, just turn the music down and switch to calmer music and the crowd will immediately relax. I'll never forget one night at my sports bar I was blasting some AC/DC late night and a group of guys started shoving each other. I quickly turned the AC/DC off and it was crazy how quickly people cooled off and walked away. Ever since then I've been a big believer in using music to help create the atmosphere I desire.

10) Pest Control

I recommend getting a licensed professional to periodically spray your establishment with pest killer approved for restaurant use.

11) Newspaper Delivery

Newspapers are nice to have at your bar, because many people come in by themselves and like to read while eating lunch or having a drink at happy hour.

12) Security (discussed in Step 14).

ONLINE RESOURCES:

1) http://www.ShortOrder.com, **1-800-211-0282**
Short Order is a great online site to purchase kitchen and bar equipment. They have buyer's guides for many equipment items you may need, such as fryers, refrigerators and freezers, convection ovens and work tables. The information provided is very useful when deciding among the wide variety of choices available.

2) http://www.CKitchen.com, **1-800-555-0666**
This site sells kitchen and bar equipment, as well as supplies. This company offers leasing options for any item that costs over $1k.

3) http://www.Centralrestaurant.com, **1-800-215-9293**
Another equipment and supply company that offers leasing.

4) http://www.usbarsupplies.com
Great source for bar and kitchen supplies, small equipment items, and janitorial supplies.

5) http://www.Samsclub.com
Sam's Club is one of my favorite spots to buy TVs and sound systems, when I can't find them used.

6) http://www.Walmart.com
I sometimes find some of the equipment and/or supplies I need at Walmart.

7) http://www.Amazon.com
Amazon has very competitive pricing on TVs, sound systems, and other equipment that's worth checking into.

8) http://www.ADP.com, **1-800-CALL-ADP ext: 411**
I've relied on ADP for my payroll services for years. Check them out, but also get quotes from at least 2 other companies as well.

9) www.BarIn30Daysorless.com
Visit the "Bar Tips" page for continually updated recommendations for online equipment and service companies to save you significant search time as well as money.

Phase 3: Construction Summary
Complete Steps in Order

Step 14: Set-Up Cameras & Alarm System
- Once you receive the necessary permits to start construction, one of the first things you will want to do is get surveillance cameras up and running to protect the building materials and equipment you start bringing in.
- Video cameras should have networking capability and should interface with the alarm system.
- Have a different code for each employee to enable/disable the alarm system in order to keep tabs on whether or not employees are acting responsibly.

Step 15: Manage Construction
- You will probably hire one if not all of the 5 specialists to construct your bar: Plumber, Electrician, Building Contractor, Painter, Audio Specialist. I save money by never hiring professional painters.
- You can hire a general contractor to manage the work and workers for you, but this can get very expensive.
- If you choose to manage the construction like I do, have a meeting with all of the contractors about what you need to get done and how you should schedule everyone so they don't get in each other's way.

Step 16: Find Equipment, Supplies, and Services
- Buying used equipment or leasing new equipment is a great way to stay on budget.
- Items to lease include Kitchen and Bar equipment, POS system, and towels/linens/door mats.
- The Kitchen and Bar equipment you choose to purchase (from *Step 12*) is up to you and your desired set-up. Some equipment items that you can't do without include a sound system with speakers, TV(s), Tables & Seating, POS system, Merchant terminal, CO_2 tank & Soda Guns, Ice Machine, Sinks.
- Services that you will need include Garbage/Grease pick up, Payroll, Accounting, Cleaning, Internet/Telephone, Electric/Gas/Water, Satellite TV/Cable, Music, Newspaper Delivery, Security.

85

Phase 4:
Late Construction

Attack Steps In Order

Step 17: Decorate

Always stay close to your core concept when you decorate. Straying away from your main idea will only cause confusion with customers. To help you decorate keep in mind what type of customers you are targeting. Do you remember that annoying saying, "birds of a feather flock to together?" Sounds silly, but it makes sense. You must decorate your establishment in line with whom you want to frequent your bar. For example if your establishment has posters everywhere of women half dressed in bikinis, you probably won't attract classy couples as customers. Or if your bar looks really modern and upscale, you probably won't have construction workers coming to your happy hour. It really doesn't matter which crowd you are trying to appeal to, just make sure you aren't pretending to be something you are not.

Regardless of what theme bar you are trying to create, focus your attention on creating a pleasant atmosphere with both décor and lighting. The bar should be inviting and have a pulled together look with a consistent theme. This should be easy to do if you keep with a consistent color theme (choose 3 main colors to incorporate) and general style throughout (i.e. old-fashioned, modern, rugged, or fancy).

Pro Tip: Try not to alarm your customer with your color choices. When choosing a color theme greens and blues always work well and provide a more relaxing effect than say a bright red or yellow.

Décor to Consider

Here are some areas to concentrate your focus on:
- *Windows:* blinds, drapes
- *Floors:* rugs, mats
- *Walls:* framed pictures, artwork, wall sconces
- *Tables/Bar/Anywhere:* vases, real and/or fake candles (there are real looking candles that have a fake flicker, which prove much safer in an atmosphere with drinking), plants (real plants can get messy, so look into attractive fake plants)
- *Behind Bar:* this is more of an operational issue than decorating idea, but keep the bottles of your beer inventory in clear view so customers don't have to waste your bartender's time by asking what you have for sale.

In the ONLINE RESOURCES at the end of this section I include the websites of some companies I use to find décor for my bars.

Staying on a Budget

Your main goal through the decorating process is to make your bar look like a million dollars, for a tenth of the cost or less. I don't care how much money you have, if you don't pay attention to costs they will get out of hand and it will take that much longer to earn a profit.

With some creativity and patience you can do a great job decorating on a low budget. One of the last bars I put together was a sports bar and I was able to put together a great looking bar for extremely cheap by purchasing over 50 different college and professional team flags online. Shopping online for different décor not only helps your budget by searching for the best prices, but it also saves the time and hassle of physically having to go to different stores.

Pro Tip: You can get a lot of free decorations for your bar from your beer and liquor distributors. Your reps have posters and sometimes (with some coaxing) can even have neon signs made for you with your bar's name on it. They have plenty of promotional items such as table tents and fruit trays that can be used in your decorating scheme. Some people feel bad asking for free stuff, but you need to do it for the sake of your budget. Besides, you give distributors business and help contribute to their salary, so ask away!

ONLINE RESOURCES:

1) http://www.Overstock.com
Overstock sells so many different décor items for very competitive pricing. You can find everything from lighting to accent rugs to framed artwork.

2) http://www.Amazon.com
Amazon sells a lot of décor items as well. They are definitely worth checking out.

3) http://www.BarIn30Daysorless.com
Visit the "Bar Tips" page to find links to online companies that great pricing on a vast array of decorations. Personally, I like shopping online because I can find good deals quickly and have everything shipped directly to my bar. Fast and efficient is always the way to go.

Step 18: Experiment with Menu & Stock Inventory

Your goal here is to get some free samples from vendors, so you can start experimenting with different items for your menu. If you really don't have any clue about cooking then I suggest you start learning right away. Like I said before you need to learn how to complete every single task to run your bar. I don't care if you have never cooked before, you can learn quickly. Cooking is all about following directions and if you have made it this far in the manual, I'm positive you can follow a recipe. At the end of this section I have included some great websites you can check for recipes to look through. I like to focus on items that are easy to prep, fairly inexpensive to stock, and always taste great.

Even if you have a tiny kitchen you should offer some sort of food menu, no matter how limited. With a few good food items, customers will stay longer and drink more, which means bigger profits! You can always create a menu that requires little or no cooking. The martini bar that I owned had a kitchen that measured around 8 ft by 4 ft, so we didn't have enough room for an oven or fryer. Instead I bought a big panini press to make gourmet sandwiches on and it was a huge hit. One of my favorite wine bars serves cheese plates with cold meats and nuts. Not only are the plates delicious, but they are extremely cheap to produce and they don't require any cooking. Obviously, if you're starting a sports bar, you won't get by with cheese plates and paninis, but don't stress. Wings, burgers, and nachos are easy enough to prep and cook just make sure you have enough variety in the beginning to determine what menu items to keep and which ones you will have to trash.

Pro Tip: Come up with a few signature menu items that no other establishments in the area carry. Not only will this make customers come to your bar because they can't get the items anywhere else, but it will create some buzz around the community and attract others to come try what you offer. Sometimes you can even charge a little extra since there is no competition. Try and take a popular drink and add your own twist to it. Maybe it's a few different ingredients, an extra large serving, or different container such as a drink served in a small fishbowl. Just get creative! In my martini bar I created a $1,000 martini that came with a diamond tennis bracelet draped over the edge and the most expensive vodka I could find. No one ever bought the martini, but just having it on the menu brought hundreds of customers through the door because so many people in the community were talking about it.

Now, get out your apron and start fixing some food! Go ahead and invite a few friends and family members to help you go through and critique what tastes good and what doesn't.

Some Easy Menu Items to Consider:
- Salads
- Wings
- Sandwiches, Paninis
- Burgers
- Pizza
- Dips: Artichoke, Guacamole, Hummus, Tzaziki, Spinach, Seafood, Salsa, Queso, Buffalo
- Nachos
- Egg rolls
- Skewers
- Soups, Chili
- Barbeque

Don't Forget Dessert

By offering a few dessert items you can add another source of revenue for you business. Most desserts are cheap to produce with high profit margin potential. Try adding fried twinkies or fried oreos to your menu. All you have to do is lightly batter the twinkies or oreos and place in your fryer for a few minutes then serve with some whipped cream or ice cream. Another easy recipe I like is cooking banana slices with some dark rum and brown sugar then serving with some scoops of ice cream. Even adding some fruit with plain vanilla ice cream can satisfy customers with a sweet tooth.

Dealing with Food Distributors

There are so many distributors to deal with in the bar business. There are distributors for beer, liquor, wine, produce, seafood, meat, dairy, and anything else you can imagine serving. I never stick with one distributor indefinitely, because every company's pricing changes from one week to the next and one might be offering a better deal than the company I used the couple weeks prior. I sometimes even buy food items from Sam's Club or Costco if they have what I need and are lower than the other distributors pricing.

Of course you want to keep a consistent product, so I never vary the quality of product I'm buying. For example if I purchase hamburger meat with an 80/20 ratio (percent lean beef to fat), I won't turn around and buy hamburger meat with a 70/30 ratio the following week, because that would change the consistency of my product. Repeat customers want to come in time and time again and get the same tasting product, so don't throw in too many changes (unless people are complaining about it in the first place).

Types of Distributors

1) Beer distributors

I usually use 3: Budweiser, Miller Lite, and a Specialty Beer company.

2) Soda distributors
The main ones to choose from are Pepsi, Coke, or a generic company. I always go with a generic company because they are always less expensive and no one can ever tell the difference.

3) Liquor/Wine distributors
In South Carolina I can have my wine delivered to me, but I have to go to the local liquor stores to purchase my liquor. The liquor stores can deliver liquor to my bar, but the actual distributor can only deliver wine. Most states allow the distributor to deliver wine and liquor, but obviously not all do.

I normally get all the juices and mixers I need from my liquor distributor as well, but you can also get your juices and mixers from your soda distributor and have them hooked up to the soda gun. The problem with hooking juices up to your gun (even though it's cheaper) is that the juice is much lower quality. If you plan on charging more for your drinks don't put juices on your soda gun.

4) Food distributors
There are so many types of food distributors out there and some companies (i.e. US Foodservice and Sysco) provide everything you might need including seafood, produce, meats, and dairy items. Depending on your area you might get better deals if you order fresh produce, seafood, and or dairy items from smaller local distributors, so try and compare pricing. Check out the ONLINE RESOURCES at the end of this section for contact information for some of the biggest food distributors.

Deciding on Inventory

The inventory needed to open varies greatly between bars. Basically it comes down to the amount of storage you have and the items you are serving. I recommend that you start with only a handful of beers, wines and liquors and slowly work your way up form there. Many bar managers assume that a larger drink selection is always better, but that's not the case.

The more you buy at the beginning the more it's going to cost you. You would be better off starting modestly and then waiting to see what your customers are going to drink. If you start off ordering a lot of everything you are going to get stuck with a lot of extras just sitting on the shelf. Just take it easy on the ordering and remember that you can always add more items as you go and you aren't required to have every single item that people request.

 Pro Tip: Regardless of what bar theme you have, make sure you carry a few alcohol and food items that are locally produced. People appreciate and enjoy local products.

Stocking Alcohol Items

The biggest part of your inventory budget will go here. Try to include a selection of vodka, rum, whiskey, gin, tequila, cognac, brandy, port, sherry, vermouth, bitters, wine cocktails, cordials, liquors, champagne, wines, draft beers, and bottled beers.

Pro Tip: Keep your liquor bottles locked up at all times in a storage closet or in the office. If the bar runs out of a bottle, the bartender must ask you or the manager for another bottle. Do not trust bar employees with your liquor inventory, you will only lose money.

Stocking Non-alcoholic Items

You need to have a selection of drinks for people who do not wish to have alcohol as well as mixers to use in the mixed drinks. Consider carrying a selection of soda and diet soda (pepsi, coke, or generic), sprite or 7-up, ginger ale, seltzer, tonic water, bloody mary mix, sweet and sour mix, grenadine, juices (orange, tomato, grapefruit, pineapple, cranberry, lime, and lemon), bottled water (sparkling and mineral), non-alcoholic beers, coffee, and tea.

Stocking Food and Food Products

If you are mainly concentrating on drinks, you should still consider buying foods that are easy to prepare for snacks or small appetizer plates (ex: assorted nuts, cheeses, cold meats, breads, chips, and/or dips). Also don't forget to order the food items you need to stock your bar such as creamer and milk, fruits (cherries, lemons, limes, oranges, pineapple, strawberries, bananas), as well as hot sauce, Worcestershire sauce, pepper, salt, olives, onions, sugar, and any other food products you need to create drinks.

Your First Order

There's no need to break the bank on your first order. Just order two bottles of everything that you are going to serve. One of the bottles will be for the bar and the other one for back up. Order your house liquors by the case (one case of each house liquor is plenty). Beer has a faster turn over rate, so I recommend buying a little more beer without overstocking too much. Only stock up before big events at your bar like before the grand opening party.

Pro Tip: Ask your distributors for discounts on products right from the beginning. They sometimes donate alcohol for opening parties and they are always running monthly specials. For example, they might run a special for ordering 50 cases of beer where you will receive $1 off per case. That might not sound like much, but every little bit helps. Remember distributors make more money when you sell and push their products, so they should be willing to help as much as needed. Don't hesitate to ask them for deals and freebies.

As for your first couple food orders, you are better off starting with a smaller supply as well. Try and order enough food inventory to last 3-5 days. Unlike your alcohol supply, your food supply can't just sit on the shelves for months and months. You will need to place a food order once or twice a week to guarantee everything is always fresh. Until you are open awhile and can gauge how much food you go through on average, start small. If you see that you are running out, place an order right away and/or run to the local grocery store to hold you over.

You can order your alcohol inventory now, but hold off on stocking your food until right before your first party (*see Step 24*). You still have to get through the hiring process and final inspections so no need to order the food just yet, it will only spoil and go to waste.

Tracking Inventory

As soon as your first inventory order arrives you must start an organized recording process. I always use a "Par Sheet" to keep track of my inventory, as well as order. You can find a copy of this sheet in the *Additional Resources* section in the back of this manual. The worksheet has 4 columns for you to keep track of what type of inventory you have, what the "par" is for that specific item, how many units you currently have in stock, as well as how many units you need to get back to par. If I've lost anyone talking about par, par is the standard unit amount of inventory that you carry in preparation for a week of business. For example, when you place your first order for house vodka your par is one case. As you get busier your par for house vodka might become 2 cases each week. For premium liquors such as Grey Goose vodka, your par might only be 2 bottles, but for Bud Light beer your par might be 25 cases. Set you par loosely at the beginning and if you find yourself running out of something increase the par for that specific item.

I always laminate my par sheet, so I can use a dry erase marker and just erase the last 2 columns each week when my inventory arrives. That way when it comes time to order again I can quickly look at supplies and fill in the last 2 columns to figure out my order.

ONLINE RESOURCES:

1) Sysco Corporation, http://www.sysco.com, **(281) 584-1390**
Sysco is one of the largest national food suppliers to restaurants and bars. Even if you don't use them as a supplier you can check out their online recipe section for recipes you may want to use.

2) U.S Foodservice, http://usfoodservice.com, **(877)-583-9659**
U.S. Foodservice is another popular national food supplier worth checking out.

3) Food Network & Allrecipes, http://www.foodnetwork.com,
http://www.allrecipes.com
2 great websites to search for recipes to use for your menu.

4) The Bar, http://www.thebar.com
This site has plenty of alcoholic and non-alcoholic drink recipes to choose from. Choose the type of liquor you want and you will find plenty of recipes. You can also do a search for drinks based on specific holidays and party themes, or even drink color.

Step 19: Price Items and Design Menus

To get started with this step compile a list of every drink and food item you plan to serve. Next, go to your competitors as well as other bars in the area and gather some menus. In order to figure out your final pricing you will need to charge somewhat close to what your competitors charge, however, depending on what type of bar you open you may get away with charging a little more or less for certain items. For example if you own a sports bar you may charge less for beer if customers purchase buckets of beer. If you own a martini bar, you may charge extra for martinis because that's your specialty.

Another factor in determining pricing is considering whom you are trying to sell to and how much they are willing to spend on a drink. Pricing too low can be as much of a problem as pricing too high, so price carefully.

Stay Consistent in the Beginning

You may tweak pricing before opening, but DO NOT change your prices in the first three months after you open. If you change the pricing you risk the chance of pushing away your initial customer base because customers expect a specific price from the bar's menu and do not like surprises on return visits. Plus you are going to have to spend money on all new menus every time you change pricing.

Food and Beverage Costs

Turning a profit in the bar industry boils down to getting food and liquor costs down to the lowest point possible. As you will see from my pricing examples to follow, I always assume that my costs are on the higher end of the spectrum. When I price food I always assume a 33% cost of the total gross profit and with alcohol I always assume a 29% cost of the total gross profit. Of course I try to get my costs down from there, but I start off with the "worst case scenario" to be on the safe side. Food profit margins are always a little less than the profit margins on alcohol, so that explains why I use a higher cost percentage estimate for food.

The Downside to Adding Taxes in Pricing

I prefer to add sales tax onto the customer's final bill, instead of including the tax into the price of drinks or food. If I include taxes in my pricing it can hurt me in the long run because on paper the government sees a larger total gross sales number and requires me to pay more income taxes on the same amount of goods sold. I will go through an example for each scenario below, so you can see exactly what I mean.

Example 1: Add tax onto each bill total, so customer pays sales tax directly.

Total Sales = $2,000
Total Sales Tax paid by customers (7%) = $2,000 x 0.07 = $140
Income Tax paid on Total Sales (33%) = $2,000 x 0.33 = $660

Total Amount Paid to the government out of my pocket = $660

Pro Tip: Spend some extra time with your POS sales representative to make sure your taxes are correctly added onto your bill.

Example 2: I include taxes in my pricing and pay sales tax to the government later.

Total Sales = $2,140 (same amount of goods sold as above, but taxes are included into pricing)
Total Sales Tax paid by me (7%) = $2,140 x 0.07 = $149.80
Income Tax paid on Total Sales (33%) = $2,140 x 0.33 = $706.20

Total Amount Paid to the government out of my pocket = $706.20+$149.80 = $856

Conclusion: My total sales amount in example 2 is more than example 1, so I wind up paying more sales tax as well as paying more income tax even though I sold the same amount of goods as in example 1.

Now if your bar slings a ton of drinks (I mean a ton) and you don't want to go through with simplifying pricing (steps below) then you can get away with pricing in example 2, I just don't strongly recommend it.

Simplify Pricing

Believe it or not, keeping the pricing simple will help your bar run more efficiently. When bartenders are slammed, a tab of $3.00 is easier to get change for than $2.96. Simplifying pricing not only helps staff members, but customers as well. Customers like to know how much they are charged each time, so it's nice if you charge simple numbers that are easy to remember.

Think about creating simple pricing on all of your drinks. Liquor is often grouped into three levels (well items, middle shelf, and top-shelf items). To keep things simple for everyone you can sell them for an even $1.00 apart. For example, for well items you might charge $3.00, middle shelf $4.00, and top shelf liquors $5.00.

You don't have to go through the following steps, but if you have a popular, constantly packed bar then it can only help with your bar's efficiency. I always figure out what the total tab amount will equal after tax is added. If you charge $3.00 for a beer and then total the tab with 6% sales tax the tab will be $3.18 (see math below).

$3.00(beer) x 0.06(sales tax rate) = $0.18 (tax)

So then……

$3.00(beer) + $0.18(tax) = $3.18 (total tab)

Now the bartender has to give out random change to the customer, which slows your bar down. Instead, let's learn to simplify the total tab price of the beer after taxes. Let's say we want a tab for one beer to equal $3.50, which would be a nice even number that will help our bartenders stay fast and efficient.

We need to figure out what we need to charge for the beer, so after tax the tab adds up to $3.50. Let's assume we have a 7% sales tax. Remember x from algebra class? Don't freak out, it's easier than you think. Here's the formula:

(Sales Tax Rate)x + 1x = $3.50 (Tab Total)

My sales tax rate is 7% (or 0.07) in this example so after I plug it into the equation it looks like this:

0.07x + 1x = $3.50

Now if you haven't had algebra for awhile, or maybe never had it don't worry! Every time you see an "x" think of it as a beer, so going back to our example….0.07x + 1x becomes 0.07 beers + 1 beers? Easy, that's 1.07 beers or 1.07x.

Now we have:

1.07x = $3.50

Now just divide $3.50 by 1.07 and you will get $3.27. This means you will have to charge $3.27 for a beer to get an even $3.50 amount on the final tab after taxes are added. Easy right? **Remember only simplify pricing on drinks, NOT FOOD!**

Obviously, simplifying pricing doesn't mean ignoring your cost and profit margins. You must go through the following steps to price your menu items and keep your costs equal to or below the appropriate levels (alcohol costs at 29% and food costs at 33%).

Determine Pricing: Liquor / Shots

1) Determine Cost per Ounce

For every bottle of liquor you serve, you need to divide the price you paid for the bottle by the number of ounces to find out the cost per ounce. For example, there are 25.35 ounces in a standard 750-ml bottle. If the bottle cost you $12, then take $12 divided by 25.35 to get the cost per ounce of $0.47.

2) Determine Shot Cost

Depending on what size shot you serve, multiply the cost per ounce (determined in step 1) by the number of ounces in the shot. Usually bars serve shots that measure anywhere from 0.75, 1, 1.5, or 2 ounces. The shot glasses you decide to stock will dictate what size shot you serve.

3) Figure price if alcohol costs are 29% of the gross sale

To make sure my costs stay at 29% or less, I divide my total shot cost by 0.29 to arrive at the price I have to charge to keep my costs in check. Since I pour 1 ounce shots I will take the cost per ounce from step 1, which is $0.47 divided by 0.29 to get $1.62. That means if I can price higher than $1.62, my costs will become less than 29%.

4) Compare with Competitor's Pricing

Take the competitor's serving size into consideration when you are comparing pricing. Their serving size may be bigger or smaller than what you plan on serving.

Determine Pricing: Mixed Drinks

1) Determine Cost of Liquor

Multiply the liquor cost per ounce (figured in step 1 above of "Determine Pricing: Liquor/Shots") by the number of ounces in the drink. Do the same thing for any other type of liquor included in the drink and then add them all together.

2) Determine Mixer Cost (plus any garnishes)

Take the total amount paid for the box or bottle of mixer (i.e. soda, juice, bloody mary mix, etc.) divided by the number of ounces to get the cost per ounce. Multiply the cost per ounce by the total number of ounces in the drink to get the total cost of the mixer in the drink.

3) Determine Total Mixed Drink Cost

Add the totals from Steps 1 and 2 plus $0.05 for drinks including soda plus garnish costs to get the total mixed drink cost.

I factor in $0.05 to the cost of every mixed drink that includes soda because I let staff members drink sodas for free and I offer free refills on soda to customers, so I factor that into the costs of my mixed drinks.

As for garnish costs, if I want to determine the cost of a lime slice I take the average price of a lime and divide it by how many slices I can get on average (8 usually) to come up with a per slice estimate. This might sound like overkill, but if you start leaving out expenses they can add up quickly and really take you by surprise. I'd rather be safe than sorry.

4) Figure Price if alcohol costs are 29% of the gross sale

I will take my total mixed drink cost (figured out in step 3) and divide it by 0.29. As an example let's say that you did the math and it costs you $1.50 to produce a Screwdriver (Vodka and orange juice). You want to make sure that the cost is 29% (max.) of your gross profit. So I'll take $1.50 divided by 0.29 to get $5.17. I must charge at least $5.17 (plus tax) for a screwdriver to keep my costs and profit margin in check. If I can get by with charging over $5.17 then I'll really be in the clear.

5) Compare with Competitor's pricing

Remember you don't want to price drinks so high that customers won't order them. Take a look at what your competitors are charging and factor that into your pricing. Let's go back to my screwdriver example. I see that my competitors charge $6.50, $8.50, and $9 for a screwdriver, so based on those numbers and the minimum I have to charge ($5.17), I figure I'll be successful charging $7.50.

Determine Pricing: Wine

1) Determine Cost per Ounce

You want to determine cost per ounce just like you did for your liquor bottles. Please see "Determine Pricing: Liquor/Shots" earlier in this section.

2) Calculate Total Cost per Serving

Multiply the cost per ounce by the number of ounces you will pour in every serving to get the total cost per serving.
3) Figure Price if alcohol costs are 29% of the gross sale

Divide the total costs by 0.29 to get the lowest dollar amount you have to charge to keep your alcohol cost at 29%.

4) Compare with Competitors Pricing

Check your competitor's pricing to see what you can get away with charging.

Determine Pricing: Beer

1) Determine Cost Per Serving

Bottles/Cans: Total cost of the case divided by the number of bottles or cans.

Draft: Cost of keg divided by number of ounces. Then multiply the cost per ounce by the number of ounces you will pour in one serving.

2) Figure price if costs are 29% of gross sale

Take the cost per serving and divide it by 0.29 to get the dollar amount you must price at or above in order to keep your alcohol cost at 29%.

3) Compare with Competitors Pricing

Compare the total to what the other bars in town are charging. Try and keep one pricing amount for all of your domestic beers and another amount for all of your imported beers.

Determine Pricing: Food

1) Figure out Cost of Menu Items

Let's say you are trying to price a burger with fries on your menu. Since you probably bought the items in bulk you first have to figure out what each part of the burger (i.e. bun, beef, cheese, etc.) will cost you. Take the total cost of the bulk item and divide it by the number of servings in each bulk package and repeat for each item you need to build your burger.

So let's pretend you come up with the following numbers (these are only examples):

1 beef patty = $0.80
1 bun = $0.30
1 slice of cheese = $0.10
Lettuce, tomato, and onion (estimated) = $0.30
1 serving of fries = $0.50

Total Cost = $2.00

2) Figure price if costs are 33% of gross sale

Now coming back to what I said earlier in this section, our food cost needs to be 33% of our gross profit (at the most). That being said I divide $2.00 by 0.33 to get $6.06. If I charge at least $6.06 (plus tax) per plate then I'll be successful in keeping my costs at 33%.

3) Compare with Competitor's Pricing

If no competitors exist, then check out pricing in other bars in the area. You want to get a feel for what customers usually pay for things. I'm still trying to price my plate of hamburger and fries, so I check with my competitors and see that they charge $8.99, $7.70, and $5.99 (all plus tax).

Now compared with what my competitors charge I think I'll be very successful charging $6.95 plus tax. This lowers my food cost even more to around 29%, which makes me happy as long as customers buy it!

An Important Question to consider:

What happens if while pricing an item, the cost causes me to price considerably higher than my competitors?

First off, you must be honest with yourself and ask, "Is my product truly better quality than my competitors?" Secondly, you should ask yourself, "Is my portion size larger?" If your product is better quality or your portion size is larger than competitors then you might be able to justify the higher price. If your product doesn't sell then you may want to tweak your product and change the price.

On the flip side, if your product is actually around the same level of quality and portion size as competitors then you must try to get costs down, because you don't want to overprice. You can get costs lower by switching to another product brand or possibly changing ingredients. If that doesn't get the cost down, then you have 3 choices. You can sell it for more than competitors and see if customers buy it, you can price it in line with competitors and accept a lower profit margin on the item, or you can just take the item off the menu altogether.

Cost Control

While we are on the subject of managing costs let's go over ways to keep costs close to or lower than the target cost percentages. Some great ways to control costs and keep a thriving business include:

1) Keeping portion sizes in check.
2) Not serving too many low profit margin food items.
3) Switching to cheaper brands without sacrificing quality.
4) Cutting out menu items that aren't selling (wasted inventory).
5) Reducing the number of menu items served (smaller inventory).
6) Taking advantage of any special promotional discounts your distributors are offering for the week or month.

When Decreasing Profit Margins can Increase Profits

Okay, so I bet you are wondering how in the world I can increase profits, but at the same time decrease profit margins? Am I crazy? No, it actually can work. Let me explain....sometimes by lowering your profit margin on one item you can attract more customers that purchase more of your other items. For example, the sports bar I owned had extremely slow Mondays and usually only netted around $800 on average. I decided to try a $2 burger promotion on Mondays, even though burgers cost me about $1.20 to produce. That meant that my food costs on my burger promotion were 60%, which was a long ways from my regular 33% target.

Within 2 weeks we were absolutely slammed on Mondays and increased our average Monday net profits to $1600. People came in for the burger deal, but also purchased fries, soda, beer, and cocktails, so decreasing my profit margin on burgers truly doubled our net profits on Monday nights.

Design Menus

The purpose of the menu is to sell food and drinks without any extra up-selling from the staff. Spending a few extra dollars on making sure the menu looks professional will definitely pay off in the long run. If you want to look at some great menu examples check out *TGI Friday's*, *The Outback*, and/or *Chili's Bar and Grille*. These guys do it right. The menus are well organized with great pictures to help up-sell the food and drink items to the customer.

So how do I make my menus? Small, simple menus create a more efficient and cost effective bar, because of 3 reasons:

1) Easier staff training
2) Less food inventory
3) Customer orders faster

Pro Tip: During the design process, talk to your distributors and ask if any of them if they want to pay to have their logo placed on your menus. This should help you offset some of the money you have to spend on menus (every little bit helps).

Common Menu Design Mistakes to Learn From

Menu Design Mistake #1: The menu is too long.

Issue: People take too long to order, because they are overwhelmed and can't figure out what they want.
Solution: Shorten the menu and keep it simple. You only need a tri-fold menu (with or without a "daily specials" insert) or a simple 11x13 inch unfolded menu. Stay away from creating a book like menu with pages and pages of items.
FYI: Many times the wine distributors provide you with the "daily specials" inserts, which will help cut down on costs.

Menu Design Mistake #2: There are no descriptions of menu items.

Issue: People don't know what they are ordering and ask too many questions, which slows down staff members.
Solution: Briefly explain ingredients, describe the food or drink item, and/or include some pictures if you wish. Pictures do a great job of up-selling menu items, especially when it comes to high profit margin specialty drinks. Make sure the pictures are taken by a photographer and not from a cheap camera or mobile phone, because if the pictures don't make your food look enticing then you are better off not using a picture.

Menu Design Mistake #3: Menu looks unorganized and unprofessional.

Issue: The customer doesn't fully trust what you sell and orders less.
Solution: Organize the menu layout into appropriate sections that are clearly labeled. For example add categorized headings like "Appetizers," "Lunch," "Dinner," "Beer," "Wine," "Cocktails," etc.

Knowing how customers scan a menu at first glance is another key factor when organizing a menu. Lucky for us, there have been studies done that prove there is a specific eye pattern when people view a menu. Customers usually look to the top left of the menu first, the bottom right portion of the menu second, the top right portion of the menu third, and the bottom left portion of the menu last. Knowing this you should have some idea of how to organize things. For example, if you want customers to go for your margarita's you should position them at the top left of your menu and not the bottom left, so they are the first menu item seen.

Menu Design Mistake #4: No strategy is used to generate maximum profits.

Issue: Menu items are placed haphazardly.
Solution: Make sure to place your highest profit margin items first and last in each menu category. It's human nature to remember and choose the first and last items of a group. For example next time you go out to eat pay close attention to the waiter's presentation of the nightly specials. Which specials are the easiest to remember? A waiter usually presents 3 to 5 specials for the evening and I think you'll find that it's always easiest to remember the first and last item.

When you place the menu items with the highest profit margins in the first and last positions of each category on the menu you increase the odds that they will sell. Another strategy to help sell your most profitable items is drawing a box around them or including small icons right next to the menu item. Both methods help certain menu items stand out from the rest. If you want to use small icons to highlight a menu item, try choosing a logo or symbol to signify the house's favorite, a pepper icon to signify a "hot" item, and/or a little red heart to signify a more health conscious item.

Ordering Menus

There are some online printing companies that have menu formatting available and all you need to do is upload your content and they will print and ship everything directly to you. Personally I'd rather save the time and money by avoiding the high costs and bad service of local printing companies. On the other hand maybe your local printing companies are better than mine.

ONLINE RESOURCES:

1) http://www.psprint.com/menu-printing, 800-511-2009
PsPrint allows you to upload your menu design and they take care of the printing. You may even hire their experts to help you with your actual menu design.

2) http://www.elance.com
You can post your menu design and printing project on Elance to have Elance professionals bid on your project.

3) http://www.uprinting.com/Restaurant-Menu-Printing.html
Another website that allows you to upload your design and have your menus printed and delivered directly to your door.

Step 20: Determine Staff Schedule and Salaries

Creating a staff schedule will also help you determine how many employees you need to hire. Let's go through the process of creating a schedule.

1) Decide on hours of operation

Your whole schedule depends on how many days of the week you are open and your hours of operation. Your hours of operation may depend on what your specific city and/ or state allows.

2) Break each day into segments

Now you may or may not be serving lunch and/or dinner so you will have to factor that into your own schedule. In my example my bar is opened 7 days a week from 11am-2am. Since I serve food at my bar my typical day is divided into the following segments:

- Lunch Prep: 10-11am
- Bar Opens: 11am
- Lunch: 11am-3pm
- Happy Hour: 4-7pm
- Dinner: 5-10pm
- Late Night: 10pm-2am
- Bar Closes: 2am
- Cleanup: 2am-3am

3) Determine the necessary staff positions

For my example, my bar is around 2,500 square feet and I have enough room in my kitchen to cook a significantly sized food menu. I need to hire workers for the following 4 positions: cook, server, bartender, and manager. Depending on your bar you might need to hire other staff members such as a bouncer(security) and/or a hostess/host.

- Cook
- Server
- Bartender
- Manager

4) Decide how many staff members you need per position during each specific time segment

The number of staff members you need will greatly depend on the size of your bar and the quantity of food you are serving. It's okay to overstaff in the beginning and if you see that you don't need as many servers on the floor and/or on the cook line then cut workers early and adjust the schedule for the following week. Overstaffing leads to high payroll costs, but being understaffed isn't good for your customer service, so it's a very delicate balance to keep your eyes on.

Pro Tip: Avoid letting your staff members overlap time on shift changes. Watch your payroll costs and have salaried positions (i.e. kitchen manager, bar manager) step in when extra assistance is needed.

5) Put together a basic plan for a typical day

Based on my needs, I've put together a schedule for my staff. Let's still assume I have a 2,500 sq. ft. venue.
10am: **Manager, Cook 1** and **Bartender 1** come in to set up, restock, and prep food.
11am: **Server 1** comes on to set up and help **Bartender 1**. **Cook 2** comes on to help with the early lunch crowd.
12pm: **Server 2** comes to help with the biggest lunch rush.
2pm-3pm: **Server 1** and **Cook 1** are cut as soon as the lunch crowd has slowed down.
4pm-7pm: **Bartender 1** may work until 4pm or sometimes until 7pm if they want to serve the happy hour crowd. **Bartender 2** comes on and cuts **Bartender 1** (at 4 or 7pm). **Server 3** comes on at 4pm to cut lunch **Server 2**. **Cook 2** is cut at 4pm when **Cook 3** comes on.
6pm: **Cook 4** comes on to assist with dinner and then stays until close because I will serve a limited food menu from 10pm-2am. **Server 4** comes on as well to serve dinner and late night cocktails and food and stays until close.
9pm: **Bartender 3** comes to assist with late night. **Server 3** and **Cook 3** are cut.
2am-3am: **Cook 4, Server 4, Bartender 3**, and **Manager/Asst. Manager** clean and close establishment.

Shift Breakdown

Server 1: 11am-2pm
Server 2: 12-4pm
Server 3: 4-9pm
Server 4: 6pm-close

Bartender 1: 10am-7pm
Bartender 2: 7pm-close
Bartender 3: 9pm-close

Cook 1: 10am-2pm
Cook 2: 11am-4pm

Cook 3: 4-9pm
Cook 4: 6pm-close

Communicating the Schedule to Staff Members
Try to have people on the same schedule week in and week out. This will make the schedule easier for everyone to remember and also save you countless hours of creating entirely new schedules each week.
Hang a bulletin board back by the kitchen or in a staff area and designate it as the "staff board". Here you will post a copy of the weekly shift schedule. Every Thursday post the following week's schedule. Attach a note on the board that reads "All requested days off must be given in writing at least 7 days in advance." Then on the side of the bulletin board have a "Request Sheet" where staff member can put their name and what date(s) they would like off from work. File these sheets so you can keep them to make the schedule for the following weeks.

Pro Tip: When I didn't have a system in place for staff to request days off it was total chaos. I can't even tell you how many times staff members would run up to me while I was in the middle of something and ask if they could have a day off and I'd say yes, but then completely forget to write it down. I would schedule them as if they never said anything and then they wouldn't show up on that day and I would be in a huge bind. Learn from my mistakes and avoid all the mess. Just let everyone know that if they don't write it down on the request sheet, their request won't be considered. To make your life even easier I suggest using an online scheduling service like Schedulefly (discussed in the ONLINE RESOURCES section below).

Setting Salaries

Obviously, you will need to pay yourself as well as your staff. Try not to pay yourself too much out of the business in the beginning until you have had a few months of success. You can always take profits later. I would recommend not paying yourself more than a couple hundred per week, unless your bar is making an absolute killing.

The manager is usually the only one on salary, because he or she is the one who is going to run most of the day-to-day operations. You can also have your manager bartend at times to cut down on payroll. As for the rest of your staff, try to pay them as little as possible. This might sound harsh, but the people in these positions are working for tips and not paychecks. In my bars in South Carolina I pay servers $2.13 per hour (plus tips), bartenders $3.00 per hour (plus tips), cooks $8-$10 per hour and managers $500-$700 per week. If I promote a bartender to assistant manager and have them take over closing duties to help my manager out, I will increase their wages to $5.00 per hour or even give them a modest weekly salary (depending on the size of the bar). If it's a bigger bar with more employees then I'm willing to pay more for the increased amount of work.

Many people argue and say that if you pay workers the minimum, they will do the very minimum amount of work to get by. I understand this philosophy, but my way has always worked for me. If an employee proves him or herself then I'm willing and eager to increase their pay, but until then, they receive the minimum. The only time when I will pay more right off the bat is if I'm trying to entice a popular, hotshot bartender in town to work for me. On rare occasions, if they are really good I will even pay them a weekly salary.

Pro Tip: Never pay overtime! You don't want to waste money on paying an employee time and a half, so never let an employee work over 40 hours a week. It's best to have the people on salary do extra work to cut out employee overtime pay.

If you are still confused about what to pay employees, the United States Department of Labor has excellent data for every state regarding average hourly wage. You can see what your state's average hourly pay is for every bar employee, including bartenders, cooks, waitstaff, hosts/hostesses, managerial positions, and many others. Please see the ONLINE RESOURCES below for the specific website address.

ONLINE RESOURCES:
1) Schedulefly, www.Schedulefly.com
Schedulefly is an extremely easy and efficient way to create shift schedules and communicate with staff members. Managers and owners logon to create staff schedules then send each staff member their personal schedule via text. Staff members also have individual online logins to communicate directly with other staff members to trade shifts, as well as request days off. It's a great way to improve communication with all the staff members and the easy interface will save you and/or your manager countless hours from manually creating the schedule every week.
The other great thing about Schedulefly is that it's relatively inexpensive. Basically, the number of employees you have will determine how much it costs you each month. If you don't mind investing a few extra dollars each month then you definitely need to give it a shot, you won't regret it.

2) United States Department of Labor – Bureau of Statistics,
http://www.bls.gov/oes/current/oessrcst.htm

This is the link to the most recent statistics compiled by the Department of Labor in regards to state wage averages. Click on your state (on the map) and then click on "Food Preparation and Serving Related Occupations" to see the occupational pay specific to the bar industry. To see what food service managers get paid on average you will have to click on "Management Occupations" after selecting your state from the map.

Step 21: Interview, Hire, and Train Staff

Start hiring and training staff members 2-4 weeks before you plan on opening your doors to the public. Like I already mentioned in the previous step, definitely plan on over hiring in the beginning. After creating the staff schedule in *Step 20,* I recommend hiring at least 20% more employees than you actually think you will need. It's definitely better to be more overstaffed then understaffed at first, because you'll have a little room to sort through which employees are good and bad for business.

The problem with initial hiring is that the dead beats in town that were recently fired from other bars are going to come straight to you. Stay on your toes and don't be surprised if after 6 months all of the initial staff members you started with are all gone. Bars have an extremely high turnover rate, that's just the nature of the business. Don't let this upset you, just expected it!

Finding Employees

Its tough to find good employees, but you will find some eventually. As long as your landlord and/or local city regulations allow, you should post a big banner outside that reads "Coming Soon," so you can start hyping up your opening. This will also catch the eye of people who are looking for work. Create a smaller sign outside your venue that reads, "Now Hiring." You can't beat free advertising right?

Your local paper and Craigslist are great advertising options as well. When people respond to your job ads have them immediately e-mail their resume. This way you can weed through people quickly without having to waste your time with lots of face-to-face interviews.

Pro Tip: One of the best ways to improve business is to recruit top employees from other hot spots around town. The most popular bartenders with the most skills are always looking to move to the newest and hottest location to make more money. Another positive is that popular bartenders usually have a customer base that will relocate to the bartender's new work location. This is a great and easy way to get customers through the door without spending extra advertising dollars.

Interviewing made easy

During the interviewing process, trust your instincts. If something doesn't make sense in a candidate's history or you feel uneasy around them just move on to the next person. Your employees are going to deal directly with your customers, so if you don't feel comfortable with your staff then your customers probably won't either.

After interviews, let candidates know that they will be called back if they indeed make the cut. People that don't hear back will sometimes still call and inquire about your decision, just them know that you found a candidate that better fits your criteria or that you are still in the interviewing process. If they probe further for a reason, stay very diplomatic and obviously avoid comments that could be considered discriminatory based on sex or race.

As for interview questions, as long as you keep them professional and appropriate the choice of questions are up to you. I normally ask the following questions and based on their answers I might ask a few more.

1) What are your strengths and weaknesses?
2) How long are looking to work here for?
3) Why should I hire you?
4) What are your career goals?
5) How did your last job end? If you are still employed, why do you want to leave your current job?
6) What type of people do you have a problem working with?
7) What type of management style do you perform best with?
8) How do you handle confrontational people?
9) Have you ever had trouble learning a new method or procedure? How did you deal with the situation?
10) How do you handle criticism?

Depending on the position I'm interviewing for I may ask to see a demonstration of skills. For example I'll ask a bartender candidate to mix me a specific drink or have a server candidate carry a few plates and drinks on a tray. I also like to incorporate some problem solving scenarios, such as "What would you do if the customer complained about a drink?" or "What would you do if the customer started acting intoxicated?"

Hiring a Manager

If you plan on hiring a manager don't make the mistake of hiring them on the first interview, no matter how great they seem. There's a lot of responsibility that goes along with this position, so you need to spend some extra time with potential candidates to make sure they are capable of doing all of the necessary tasks in a highly efficient manner. I recommend interviewing candidates at least 3 times before making a final decision.

Since the manager plays such a crucial role in your day-to-day operations make sure they are compensated well with added benefits such as health insurance. Managers can easily burn out from the hectic long hours, so I always like to include added incentives. For example I may offer a pay bonus if they bring in so much revenue per night or if they keep operating costs under a certain level for 3 months in a row. I also sometimes give managers the opportunity to earn a percentage of actual ownership if they perform their job successfully for 6 months in a row.

If you choose to personally take on the role as an active manager, I recommend promoting the head bartender to assistant manager to help open and close the bar at times. As manager you can clock in as many as 50-70 hours a week, so it's nice to try and have an assistant to close the bar and complete the daily reports. Even if you do hire a manager, you still might want to provide them with a little relief and promote the head bartender to assistant manager.

Employee Forms

Once you hire any staff member have them fill out the following documents before they start.

1) Hiring Document

I recommend that you create a hiring document for each position in your bar (i.e. server, bartender, manager, cook, etc.). Basically the hiring document is an agreement that states the employee has read the employee manual (I will come back to this in a minute) and understands the rules of the establishment and key responsibilities for their specific position as well as salary description. Have each employee sign this document before they begin work.

Whenever someone breaks a rule or doesn't do their job, the hiring document is proof that everything was presented to them when they were hired. When they insist and say, "You never told me that," just pull out their hiring document and show them where they signed their name. If an employee violates one of my rules then I record the date, time, and type of violation in their employee file. I have a 3 strikes you're out rule policy, which means employees have 3 chances before I decide it's time to let them go. If they do something like steal from me, act offensively towards a customer, or get intoxicated at my bar then I have no problem firing them immediately.
Please visit the *Additional Resources* section at the back of this manual for examples of hiring documents for bartenders, cooks, servers, and managers. The employee duties will probably vary at your bar, but you can use mine as a general guideline.

2) Two Government Forms (I-9 and W-4)

Along with having your new hire sign a hiring document there are a few other mandatory forms they have to fill out as well. You will need to have them fill out an I-9 Employment Verification Form as well as a W-4 Form. You can usually buy these forms at places like OfficeMax or you can print them for free from the links located in the ONLINE RESOURCES at the end of this section. Make sure you always use the forms for the current year. Just make a note to yourself that every November you should get the new forms for the upcoming year.

Place all of the signed documents as well as a copy of the employee's driver's license and social security card into a separate file for each employee and keep these files for 5 years. Even if an employee only works for a few days, it's in your best interest to hold onto their file for a while. Lawsuits and other bogus charges can surface from employees you barely remember, so keep employment records long after the employee is gone.

When to Have Background Checks Done

I don't waste my time doing background checks on any employees other than potential managers. When hiring managers I always check references as well as have criminal background checks done. Nowadays you can get accurate background checks done online. It does cost a little money, but not much considering the money you could lose if you hire the wrong person. I honestly believe it's worth every penny. Check the ONLINE RESOURCES at the end of this section for some recommended companies.

Unfortunately I didn't always perform background checks, so I had to learn the hard way. I once hired a manager and over the course of time found bottles of liquor disappearing and faulty record keeping of profits. I found out later that my manager had 3 DUIs on his permanent record. If I had only done the proper investigating beforehand I would never in a million years hired him to be in charge of one of my bars. Hopefully you won't make the same mistake.

Pro Tip: Once you hire your staff members try to get them to help you out with decorating and putting the finishing touches on the bar. Having your employees involved in getting the bar up and running helps save money by not having to pay expensive contractors. Most of the time employees will be happy to help out, because they figure they might score better hours if they help out a little and guess what? It's true! I can really tell which employees are motivated and ready to succeed and I will definitely give those employees first dibs on the hours they want.

Create an Employee Manual

Contrary to popular belief an employee manual doesn't have to be long winded. If it's too long then employees will never read it anyway. I recommend at least addressing your stance on the important issues listed below:

- Goals of venue
- Breaks during shifts
- Trading shifts with co-workers and requesting time off
- Payroll schedule

- Hours of operation and Holidays / Days closed
- Behavior and performance expectations
- Tardiness policy
- Customer service expectations
- Uniform and hygiene rules
- Drinking / eating on the job
- Dating co-workers
- Staff parking
- Staff discounts
- Food Safety
- Hazard Reporting
- Fire Safety
- Cleaning Procedures
- Sexual Harassment
- Stealing / Giving away drinks and food
- Personal cell phone use
- Operation procedures
- Opening and Closing procedures

After you hire staff members let them know that when their training is complete they will be tested on their knowledge. Employees should be tested either through a written or oral test. This should let them know you mean business and that they MUST pay attention and learn the material.

Train Staff

After you hire staff members, spend time training and training some more. Your staff needs to learn everything from how to stock the bar, to cleaning up properly, to knowing how to up-sell customers.

The more time you spend training the staff the better they will be at making you money. A great example of a business with excellent training is *The Outback*. We all know that *The Outback* runs a great business, but what you probably didn't know is that their employees have to go through 2 weeks of intensive training before they can even start as a server.

In the past I made the mistake of expecting staff members to remember everything the very first time I said it. As you probably can guess, this doesn't work well and it only leaves you frustrated and annoyed. You have to put yourself in your employee's shoes and repeat information over and over to engrain details in their memory. Afterwards have them repeat things back to you and quiz them on what they have learned. Without excessive training you can't expect your staff to know how to get the job done the way you want.

I recommend having a mandatory staff meeting every week even if it's brief. These meetings are a good time to go over any problems and/or successes that have occurred as well as review different promotions for the upcoming week. If you had an issues with a specific employee arrange a separate meeting with them away from the group. The weekly staff meeting is not a good time to single people out, unless it's to offer praise for a job well done.

Have an Operating System In Place

The bottom line in training and operations is that you MUST be systematic. For every single task in your bar you need to verbally explain and write down the **what, when,** and **how**. Employees need to know **what** they need to do, **when** they need to do it, and exactly **how** it MUST be done. Instructions need to be absolutely crystal clear, so other interpretations aren't even possible. Posting task lists and pictures of how you want things to look are excellent ways to help guide staff members.

To help you develop a strong system for staff operations I recommend reading "The E-Myth," by Michael Gerber. Gerber has a whole series of books for small business owners on how to organize your operations for success.

Specific Training for Certain Staff Members

Servers Must learn the following:
- Different types of alcohol and the corresponding glassware used.
- Customer service skills and up-selling.
- Protocol for handling difficult customers.
- Expected frequency and time intervals of checking on customer.
- Signs for when a customer should be cutoff from alcohol.
- Taking orders and properly entering them into the POS.
- Proper clean-up.
- The basics of food/drink delivery and where to stand at the table.
- Handling customer payment.
- Menu items and pricing.
- Opening and closing procedures.

Bartenders Must learn the following:
- How drinks should be prepared and how they should look.
- Customer service skills and up-selling.
- Signs for when a customer should be cutoff from alcohol.
- Protocol for handling difficult customers.
- Proper usage of equipment and supplies.
- Taking orders and properly entering them into the POS.

- Keeping track of bar inventory.
- Measures to reduce costs and limit waste.
- Proper clean-up and storage of leftover food products and alcohol.
- Handling customer payment.
- Menu items and pricing.
- Opening and closing procedures.

Cooks Must learn the following:
- Safe food handling.
- How menu items should be prepared and how they should look.
- Keeping track of food inventory.
- Proper measures to reduce costs and limit waste.
- Label and store inventory in the appropriate ways.
- Know how to sanitize equipment and supplies.
- Proper clean-up and storage of leftover food products.
- Procedures for heating, re-heating, cooling, and freezing.

More Staff Training You Can't Ignore

Besides training staff members on operations specific to their positions you must focus time on the following training that effects the bar industry:

1) Alcohol Laws Training
Contact the state agency responsible for alcohol law enforcement for a complete guide to alcohol laws (see the "Additional Resources" section in the back of this book for state agency contact information). Some state departments offer training programs and testing supplies for bar staff. Another resource for training your staff is a manual called *The Responsible Serving of Alcoholic Beverages: A Complete Staff Training Course for Bars, Restaurants, and Caterers.* You can find it through Atlantic Publishing (800-814-1132).

2) Food & Beverage Training
Measures must be taken to produce food and drink products with customer safety in mind. Staff members should learn how to handle, prepare, and serve food items in a way that prevents contamination and improves quality. Even if you aren't serving much food on your menu staff members still handle food products when creating drinks, so don't ignore this training.

3) Sexual Harassment Training
Sexual harassment is an issue in every work environment, but when you add alcohol into the mix you can really have problems if you aren't careful. Staff members must know what behavior is unacceptable and how they should handle inappropriate behavior from customers.

4) Emergency Training
All employees should learn emergency procedures. If a staff or customer chokes, a robbery occurs, or a fire starts, your employees need to know what's expected of them.

ONLINE RESOURCES:

1) Craigslist, http://www.craigslist.org
Craiglist is a great place to post job openings for your bar.

2) I-9 Form (PDF file), http://www.uscis.gov/files/form/i-9.pdf; **W-4 Form (PDF file),** http://www.irs.gov/pub/irs-pdf/fw4.pdf
2 forms that must be filled out by every new employee.

4) http://www.uscis.gov/portal/site/uscis
This website contains a lot of useful information for employers.

5) Intelius, http://www.intelius.com; **USSearch,** http://www.ussearch.com
2 great website for employers to get background checks done on job applicants, fast and simple.

Step 22: Complete Budget and Breakeven Report

You must set a budget before you even open. Of course this budget will change, but having a layout to start with makes life that much easier down the road. I recommend using a monthly budget system and from there you can always figure out a weekly and then daily budget if needed. A monthly budget system should list your reoccurring costs (i.e. electric, payroll, sewer, rent, internet, TV service, etc.), as well as any one-time expenses (i.e. equipment and/or supplies).

In the beginning you'll need to review your budget every few days to make sure you are staying on track. Money can flow out of your pockets like water if you don't keep track of your expenses very closely.

Getting in the habit of evaluating your expenses on a regular basis will help you recognize drastic changes from the prior week or month, which will help you identify and correct any potential problems early.   Believe me, you want to do everything you can to eliminate losing money along your journey.

Budgeting Rule of 1/3

Budgeting involves not only watching expenses, but also managing profits. The best way to measure whether you are budgeting successfully is to remember the Rule of 1/3:

- 1/3 of your budget will go toward inventory costs for food, beer, wine, and liquor.
- 1/3 goes towards operating costs and one-time expenses.
- 1/3 will go in your pocket. If you are able to keep 1/3 of the money that comes across the bar then you are running a great business.

When do you make time to budget?

I know that you're probably thinking, "How the heck am I going to find time to budget when I have a million other things to do?" Well, I'm sorry to break the news to you, but in order to be successful in this business you must budget on a regular basis. At the end of every month I balance my books and see where I am in regards to profits and expenses. This not only let's me know if I'm in the red or black for the month, but also helps me get organized for quarterly taxes.

On a daily basis I log my total sales from the day prior and see how the bar performed in regards to the daily break even point. The break even point is crucial in measuring your level of success everyday, so we will discuss this more over the next few pages. I usually take care of my budgeting and sales recording each morning, because I can work in peace and quiet and enjoy a cup of coffee before anyone else comes into the bar. Trying to get financial matters done during business hours is nearly impossible. Most bar owners use Quickbooks to budget, so that might work better for you than writing it down manually like I do.

The Break Even Point

The break even point is the amount of money you must strive to exceed on a daily basis to cover your expenses and take profits. Any amount over your daily break even point is pure profit. If your daily performance falls below your break even then you better work hard to lower expenses (if possible) and increase profits. Of course you will have days where you don't hit your break even, but work to make these days few and far between. If you can beat this number on a regular basis then you are well on your way to success.

You don't need to be up and running to figure out your break even point. As long as you have some quotes for expenses you can figure out an estimate for your daily break even number. Take a look at the example of a Break Even Report on the following pages as well as the step-by-step explanation, which guides you through creating one.

BREAK EVEN REPORT (example)

Part A: Total Expenses	Yearly ($)	Monthly($)
Accounting	500.00	41.66
Promotions	3,000.00	250.00
Utilities	2,200.00	183.33
Insurance	6,000.00	500.00
Licenses	425.00	35.41
Office	1,800.00	150.00
Postage	148.00	12.33
Rent	8,400.00	700.00
Repairs	3,600.00	300.00
Supplies	7,200.00	600.00
Payroll (see parts B & C)	**144663.84**	**12055.32**
Cable	1,500.00	125.00
Telephone	1,100.00	91.66
Internet	500.00	41.66
Security System	480.00	40.00
Trash	1,800.00	150.00
Advertising	8,400.00	700.00
Employee Tax	31,825.72	2,652.14
Bank Fees	2,030.00	169.16
Payroll Processing Fees	500.00	41.66
Auto	750.00	62.50
Entertainment	4,000.00	333.33
Laundry	800.00	66.66
Misc.	6,500.00	541.66
TOTAL	**238122.56**	19843.48

Break Even Report (cont.)

Part B: Total Employee Hours	Year	Month	Week	Day
Bartender 11am-12am	4368	364	91	13
Server 1 11am-3pm	1344	112	28	4
Server 2 11am-2pm	1008	84	21	3
Server 3 5pm-11pm	2016	168	42	6
Kitchen 1 prep 8-2	2016	168	42	6

Kitchen 2 11am-5pm	2016	168	42	6
Kitchen 3 5pm-12	4704	392	98	14
Asst Mgr	salaried	position		
MGR	salaried	position		

PART C: **Total Staff Payroll**	**Yearly ($)**	**Monthly ($)**	**Weekly ($)**	**Daily ($)**	**Hourly Pay Rate**
Bartender	13104.00	1092.00	273.00	39.00	$3.00
Server 1	2862.72	238.56	59.64	8.52	$2.13
Server 2	2147.04	178.92	44.73	6.39	$2.13
Server 3	4294.08	357.84	89.46	12.78	$2.13
Kitchen 1	17136.00	1428.00	357.00	51.00	$8.50
Kitchen 2	17136.00	1428.00	357.00	51.00	$8.50
Kitchen 3	39984.00	3332.00	833.00	119.00	$8.50
Asst Mgr	19200.00	1600.00	400.00	N/A	N/A
MGR	28800.00	2400.00	600.00	N/A	N/A
TOTAL	**144663.84**	**12055.32**	3013.83	N/A	N/A

Break Even Report (cont.)

Part D	**Yearly ($)**	
Total Expenses	238122.56	
Food and Alcohol Costs (33%)	78580.44	{Total expenses (238122.56) x .33}
Total Yearly Cost Estimate	316703.00	

Daily Break Even Pt. = Total Costs ($316,703)/Days Open per Year (365)

Daily Break Even Pt. = $867.68

Steps to creating a Break Even Report

1) Create a new excel spreadsheet program on your computer. If you don't have excel then a simple paper and pencil will work.

2) As shown in Part A, create a column that categorizes every possible expense. Use my list as a guideline, but add/subtract some categories depending on your own bar's expenditures. Remember that some expenses are reoccurring while others are only a one-time expense.

3) For each expenditure on your list go ahead and estimate a monthly/yearly amount. Before you add up your total expenses in Part A, we must first move onto Part B and C to calculate an estimate for total payroll costs.

4) As shown in Part B, you must figure out how many hours each staff position works. List each position and record the total hours the specific position works per day. For example, even though my bar has a few bartenders, I only pay hourly wages for the bartender position for 13 hours per day (from 11am to 12am I keep one bartender working). My salaried employees (assistant manager and manager) help assist the bartender.

As you can see in the far right hand column of Part B, you must add how many hours in a day each position works (far right column) then multiply that number by 7 (based on staying open 7 days a week) to get the total weekly hours. Next, multiply the total weekly hours by 4 to get the total monthly hours estimate. And finally, multiply the monthly number by 12 to get the total yearly hours estimate.

5) For Part C use the data gained in Part B to figure out how much money is paid to employees. Take the hourly wage for each employee and multiply by the number of hours the position works per day (in my example, the manager and assistant are on salary so pay per hour doesn't for them apply). For example, for the bartender position I pay $3.00 an hour and since the bartender position will work 13 hours a day, I multiply $3.00 by 13 hours (I use the chart in Part B to help) to arrive at $39. That means I spend $39 per day on bartender payroll. When I want to figure out how much I pay bartenders per week I take $3.00 then look in Part B to find out the number of hours I owe for the week (91) then multiply the two to get the amount of $273 for the week. This is what I go through to figure out the total amount paid to each staff position for the day, week, month, and yearly time frame.

6) In Part C, add each staff position's salary to get a total payroll amount for each time frame. Take the monthly and yearly totals and plug them back into the "Payroll" expenditure item that we left blank in Part A.

7) In Part A, go ahead and add up all of the expenses to get a final total for your Yearly and Monthly expenditures.

8) Proceed to Part D where we need to calculate food and alcohol costs and add them into our grand total. Here, I take the Total Yearly Expenses (figured in Part A) and multiply by 0.33 (or 33%) to determine an estimate for food and alcohol costs. Like I explain in *Step 19*, I know that if I can keep my food costs at 33% (or lower) and alcohol costs at 29% (or lower), I will have a better chance of succeeding. I choose to calculate a food and alcohol estimate with 33%, so I can plan for the "worst case scenario."

9) Take the total food and alcohol costs estimate and add it onto your total yearly expenses from Part A to get a new yearly cost total estimate that includes food and alcohol.

10) Take the new total calculated in the last step and divide it by the number of days that you are open per year. If you are open 7 days a week including holidays, then this step should be very easy (divide by 365). If not, make sure you subtract each day you plan on staying closed from 365 and then divide by the total. This final dollar amount is your daily break even point.

Pro Tip: No need to worry if your business doesn't hit your break even point on a regular basis for the first month or two of being open. Keep your focus on growing your business by improving operations, out-performing the competition, and increasing marketing efforts. The profits will come if you keep working the right way, so don't stress about cutting costs too much at the very beginning.

Step 23: Schedule Final Inspections

In order to open your doors to the public your bar needs to pass all of the necessary final inspections for your city and state. Before you schedule the inspections make sure that construction is finished and you have all the necessary equipment and supplies needed to take care of customers. Since you probably had workers moving in and out of your property the last few weeks you need to do a final cleaning. The floors should be cleaned and all countertops and tables should be given a final wipe down to get rid of any extra dust or dirt that accumulated during the hectic construction phase.

At this time you should do a final check on the flow of your bar as well. Now that you have your tables, chairs, and equipment, analyze whether or not it's easy to move around your bar. Is the layout efficient for staff operations and appealing to customers? You can bring a few friends in and get their feedback if you don't know where to place things. Sometimes when you see the same thing everyday you can have the tendency to look past certain issues, so bringing in a fresh set of eyes never hurts.

As I touched on earlier, each State has different inspections that your bar needs to pass before you can open. Refer back to *Step 10* for a list of departments you must contact to find out specific city/state requirements. For example in South Carolina a Food and Beverage establishment needs to be cleared by the Fire Marshall, Building Inspector, SLED (South Carolina Law Enforcement Division), and DHEC (South Carolina Department of Health and Environmental Control) before opening.

The Fire Marshall inspection and Health inspection are pretty standard across the board so let's go a little more in depth on both.

Fire Marshall Inspection

The Fire Marshall not only checks to see whether your establishment is up to fire code with properly marked exits and fire extinguishers, but they also determine your occupancy rating. The occupancy rating is the maximum allowance of people you may have in the bar at any given time. Be polite to the Fire Marshall and follow him or her through your establishment as they go through. Normally inspectors are less thorough when they are being watched. Hopefully you contacted them back in *Step 11*, so they already know you care about their inspection and have addressed their previous concerns.
You can get in trouble with the Fire Marshall down the road if you have a small bar and pack in lots and lots of people (something that I love to do). One of my small Irish bars

had a record turnout for St.Patrick's Day one year and the Fire Marshall showed up the next day and gave us a warning. I found out later that the bar owner down the street called to complain. I made sure I went to his bar for a drink every once and awhile, so he wouldn't call the authorities on me again and luckily we never had another complaint.

Pro Tip: The type of bar you want to open should dictate whether or not you want to secure a higher or lower occupancy rate. I push for lower occupancy rates when I open a bar with a big focus around sporting events. Now why would I do that? The reason is that many satellite TV companies charge for pay-per-view sporting events based on occupancy rates. For a venue with a higher occupancy rate they can charge as much as $500 extra for a single pay-per-view event. If you aren't going to have many sporting event parties at your bar then there's no reason why you wouldn't want a higher occupancy rate. That way you can pack in larger crowds without the risk of getting into trouble.

Health Inspection

The health inspection is another inspection that every establishment must go through. As with all inspections you will want to have everything clean and sparkling. I recommend mopping the kitchen floor and area behind the bar with some Pine-sol about 30 minutes prior to their arrival, so your establishment has a fresh, clean smell to match it's appearance (just make sure it's dry by the time the inspector gets there). You want to make sure the health inspector has a great first impression when he or she walks through the door.

Over the years I have put together a checklist derived from other organizations that provides a guideline for not only getting my bars ready for inspections, but also for operating safely on a day to day basis. Depending on your city and state you may need to add some other requirements as well.

Checklist for Inspections and Safety

Restaurant and Food Operations:

1) Kitchen waste materials (grease) stored in metal containers with tight-fitting lids.
2) Operable automatic extinguishing system in hood and duct above ranges, grills and fat fryers.
3) Extinguishing system's manual pull switches located away from cooking equipment.
4) Fuel supply for cooking equipment has an automatic shut-off valve when extinguishing system activates.
5) Deep-fat fryer units controlled and provided with high-temperature shut-offs; overflow gutters provided.
6) Filters in exhaust system(s) cleaned.

7) Floors adjacent to deep-fat fryers dry and free of grease.
8) Floors adjacent to soda guns cleaned.
9) Floors around sink mopped dry.
10) FRP properly placed.

Fire Protection and Prevention:

1) Proper number and type(s) of fire extinguishers, charged and tagged to show last service date.
2) Fire extinguishers properly wall-mounted, identified and adequately accessible for hazard involved.
3) Employees trained in proper use of extinguishers and manual operation of system protecting cooking equipment.
4) If there is a sprinkler system, a minimum of 18 inches clearance between stock storage and sprinkler heads.
5) Clear space of three feet around sprinkler system's main control valve available.
6) Sprinkler system(s) periodically tested and maintained; written records kept on premises.
7) Instructions prominently posted for reporting fire and calling Fire Department.
8) Flammable and combustible liquids (paints, solvents, etc.) stored in metal safety cabinets or off premises.
9) Storage of combustibles away from furnaces or other heat source.

Electrical Equipment

1) All electrical equipment properly grounded.
2) Breaker switches properly marked.
3) Electrical panel boxes have doors closed, clear area of 30 inches in front of boxes.
4) Switches, switch boxes, outlets and wiring inspected periodically and deficiencies corrected.

Storage Areas

1) Inventory properly and securely stacked.
2) Good housekeeping maintained, aisles clear, storage orderly, floors free of debris, storage has proper clearances from hot-water heater and sprinklers.
3) Shelving and racks in good repair and secured to avoid tipping.

Cold-storage and Refrigeration Equipment

1) Refrigeration and air-conditioning compressors clean, well ventilated, kept clear of combustibles.
2) Walk-in cooler and freezer doors provided with operable interior-release mechanisms, alarm system, and axe.

Floors and Walking Surfaces

1) Floor free from food spillage, silverware, broken glassware, loose mats, torn carpets or other hazards.
2) Portable signs available to indicate wet-mopped floors or temporary hazards.
3) Stair treads equipped with abrasive strips or other nonskid surface.
4) Outdoor walkways checked frequently for, tripping hazards; repairs made promptly.
5) Indoor-outdoor carpeting or other type of mat provided at entrance doors.
6) Changes in interior floor levels properly illuminated.

Exits

1) Exits properly marked, illuminated and unobstructed; doors kept unlocked during hours of operation or equipped with panic bars.
2) Non-exit doors (to rest room area, kitchen, closets, etc.) identified properly.

Exterior Areas

1) Paths and parking lot well illuminated.
2) Steps, ramps, grounds, parking lot in good repair, free of holes or obstruction, well illuminated.
3) Snow and ice promptly removed from parking lot and all walkway surfaces, when necessary.

General Safety Practices

1) Pest control services performed by a licensed, independent extermination contractor. The substances used must be approved for use in food establishments.
2) Heimlich Maneuver posters in plain view; employees trained, where required by law.
3) Fully equipped first-aid kit available at all times.
4) Emergency telephone numbers for police and emergency medical services prominently posted.
5) Dishes and utensils taken out of service and discarded if chipped, cracked and/or broken.

Phase 4: Late Construction Summary
Attack Steps in Order

Step 17: Decorate
- Stay with your core concept and use the overall design to appeal to the type of customer you want to attract.
- Stick with a consistent color theme when decorating.
- Online shopping for decorations helps to compare prices quickly and saves time by not having to physically go to stores.
- See what decorations your distributors can give you for free.

Step 18: Experiment with Menu & Stock Inventory
- Get free food samples from vendors and recruit friends and family members for a taste test.
- Limiting yourself to a few simple menu items can help cut down on inventory costs and help you focus on your biggest profit margin items....alcoholic drinks!
- Ordering less in the beginning will give you time to determine what's popular with your customers before you spend a lot of money.
- A bigger selection of products is not always better, things might end up sitting on the shelf and that equals lost money.
- You need to order from beer distributors, soda distributors (I always use generic), liquor/wine distributors and food distributors.
- Ask the distributors for weekly/monthly promotional deals and go with the distributors that offer the best price. You don't have to stick with the same distributor every week or month. I jump around to get the best deals.

Step 19: Price Items and Design Menus
- You need to keep your food and alcohol costs at a maximum of 33% of your total profit. Alcohol should be a little lower than food (29% as opposed to 33%).
- Simplifying pricing helps your bar's efficiency as well as your customers.
- Go through the necessary steps to figure out the cost of each drink and food item you serve, in order to price accurately.
- Always compare your pricing to other bars in the area, so you aren't over or undercharging.
- If your price is much higher than your competitors then you have to research whether your price is justified.
- Decreasing a profit margin for a special promotion can sometimes increase profits.
- Your menu needs to sell your products all on it's own. Spending a little extra dough here is worth it.
- Small menus are great because they equate to easier staff training, less food inventory, and faster customer ordering.

Step 20: Determine Staff Schedule and Salaries

- Creating a schedule helps determine how many employees to hire.
- When creating a schedule, first decide on hours of operation. Second, break the day down into segments (i.e. Lunch prep 11am-12pm, Lunch 12-2pm, Happy Hour 4-7pm, etc.). Third, figure out what positions you need to staff. Lastly, decide how many staff members you need in each position during each specific time segment.
- Overstaff shifts in the beginning and make adjustments as you go.
- Make sure shift changes are made quickly.
- Don't let staff members work overtime.
- Have an iron proof system in place for scheduling and requesting days off.

Step 21: Interview, Hire, and Train Staff

- Hire 2-4 weeks before you open the doors for your first party.
- Overstaff by at least 20% in the beginning to weed out the bad employees.
- When hiring a manager never hire them on the first interview. Meet with them at least 3 times before you make your decision and spend the extra money on a background check.
- Hiring documents are proof that the employee understands their responsibilities as well as the rules and regulations of your bar.
- New hires must complete a I-9 and W-4 form.
- Creating an employee manual helps the employees understand where you stand on important issues. Even if you type up a single page of important rules, it's better than none.
- Spend time training your staff right. They need to know what they need to do, when they need to do it, and how it must be done! Don't assume they know how to do anything!

Step 22: Complete Budget and Breakeven Report

- Keep an eye on where your money is going. Numbers don't lie so if you see expenses growing greatly, look into the underlying issue further.
- The Budgeting Rule of 1/3 states that a 1/3 of your budget goes toward inventory costs (food, beer, wine, and liquor), 1/3 goes toward operation costs and one time expenses, and the last 1/3 goes in your pocket.
- You MUST figure out your Break Even number, so you know how much you have to gross each day to cover expenses.

Step 23: Schedule Final Inspections

- As soon as your bar is set-up and ready to host your first party, go ahead and schedule final inspections (from your research in *Step 10* you should know what departments you need approval from).
- Before inspections your bar should be spotless.

Phase 5: Open to the Public

Attack Steps 24 & 25 Simultaneously

Step 24: Plan an Opening Strategy

You should progress through a few stages before you begin heavy advertising and planning for a grand opening party. Oftentimes, new bar owners rush through opening and major problems follow. Staff underperforms, operational issues arise, customers have an awful first impression, and money is lost. If you open in a hurry, your establishment might never recover. Let's map out the 4 events that should lead you to your final opening.

1) The Friends and Family Party

Before you open your doors to customers, throw a party for your closest friends and family members in order to have them test your menu items as well as give you and your staff some practice. Friends and family are more accepting of imperfections (usually) than the general public, so it should be a great stress free environment for you and your staff to learn in.

During the party keep an eye on how the staff performs and give them some advice along the way to help them improve what they are doing. Place comment cards all over the bar and have your staff push your guests to fill them out with anything that they have suggestions on. The comment cards should give valuable feedback as to what aspects you and the staff members need to focus and improve on.

Even though the friends and family party is usually a very relaxed event, this is no time for the staff to relax. This is test day and you need to see how everyone performs, so make sure everyone understands the main goal of the night.

The day following the friends and family party you can move onto the 2 week soft opening phase.

Family & Friends Party summary:
- **Purpose:** Test menu items and give staff members practice.
- 25 people maximum.
- 2 hours in the evening.
- All food/drinks are free (only serve house liquors and beer).
- Have staff hand out comment cards to guests.
- Stock food inventory so you are ready for the Soft Opening to follow.

2) The Soft Opening

The soft opening refers to the first 2 weeks of being open to the public for normal business hours; however, you are not going to advertise and market that you are open quite yet. You may place a sign outside your establishment that reads "Open," but keep the other marketing hype to a minimum. The main purpose of the soft opening is to help you and the staff members solve operating issues before becoming too busy with customers. It's amazing how much can go wrong and what aspects you forgot to account for sometimes. Towards the end of the 2-week soft opening period plan on throwing an invitation only party.

Soft Opening Summary:
- **Purpose:** Work out operational issues, before becoming too busy.
- The bar is open to the public with normal business hours.
- Charge regular prices.
- No advertising besides an "Open" sign (you want customers, but not too many).
- Plan the invitation only party to follow the soft opening.

3) The Invitation Only Party

For the invitation only party you should send out invitations to anyone that had a hand in helping you open your bar. Invite everyone, including the town Mayor, Police Chief, Fire Marshall, Fire Department, Chamber of Commerce, and City Hall members. This helps get everyone behind you from the very beginning.

Try and limit your guest list to between 50-100 people. Create a 4x6 invitation that you can hand them out as well as mail. Have the party for only 2 hours in the early evening and serve free domestic beers, house liquor, as well as food samples of menu items that you plan on serving. If you are not serving food then you can always have some snacks or catered appetizers available. After the 2 hours people must pay for drinks. The event should not cost you very much and people always want to stay after the party ends, so expect to make a little money by the end of the night.

Invitation Only Party Summary:
- **Purpose**: Introduce your bar to important members of the community to stir up some interest.
- Limit between 50-100 guests.
- Invite important people in town as well as friends.
- Serve 2 hours of free domestic beers, house liquors, and food samples.
- Guests must pay for premium/top shelf alcohol and imported beers during the party.
- After 2 hours is up, no more freebies from the bar

4) The Grand Opening Party

A month after your invitation only party you should host a grand opening party. You will want to heavily market this event to ensure a great turnout. Write a short press release about your bar and send it to all the local newspapers as well as magazines. Just call the different media offices and ask whom you can send a copy of your press release to. The press release only needs to be a few sentences long, just make sure you include the name of your bar, what type of bar it is, why it's unique, and the date of the party. This way you can get word out about your opening for free, because local newspapers and magazines are always looking for new stories. Press releases often stir more interest and in depth stories down the road as well, which is great for marketing.

Another way to get the word out about your opening is to attend local networking events and/or popular public areas where you and a few friends can hand out flyers and talk to others about your new bar opening. I often go to local businesses and other restaurants and bars to invite people into my grand openings. The bottom line is don't leave it to others to find out about your bar on their own. Go out into the community and create some buzz! People love checking out new bars so don't be shy!

For the party, consider hiring a popular local band or musician to perform. This will not only help entertain customers, but good bands usually come with a group of people that enjoy their music, so they can help ensure a larger crowd.

The day of the party place a huge sign or banner out front that reads "Grand Opening", so people passing will easily be able to see. One of your distributors might make this sign for you for free if you ask nicely, so check with them before you buy one.

For the party you can advertise a promotion on drinks or food, but by no means should you give away anything free like you did for your other parties. Now is the time to take profits!

Grand Opening Party Summary:
- **Purpose:** Introduce your bar to the entire community and start making big profits!
- You should host this party 1-month after the Invitation Only Party.
- Heavily market the event.
- No free food/alcohol giveaways, but you can have a promotion if you choose.
- Party will run from evening until close.
- Hire entertainment.
- See what freebies your distributors will donate for your big event.
- Make sure you are well stocked with the essentials (i.e. beer and liquor) for the big party.

Step 25: Begin Marketing Plan

You shouldn't do much heavy marketing until you get closer to your grand opening party, but that doesn't mean you can't start setting a marketing plan right away.

From the very beginning, concentrate on growing your list of contacts so you can promote your business to as many people as possible. For example, as soon as you are open to the public have a weekly raffle giveaway where customers leave business cards to enter to win a gift certificate. If you concentrate on obtaining as many people's names, e-mails, and cell phone numbers as you can, you will have a good start when you launch your marketing campaigns.

Your time and energy should focus around 3 marketing campaigns: Internet, Mobile, and Local.

Internet Marketing Campaign

1) Website

Nowadays you can't ignore the powerful influence of the internet. Thousands of people search the web to find bars and restaurants, so if you don't have a web presence you'll miss out on a great source of new business. Even existing customers like to browse menus and view upcoming events and parties, so it's important that you have something online to promote your business further.

Many people don't have websites mainly because they think it's too expensive and if you hire someone locally, it probably would be. If you are smart you won't go that route. Here's what you need to do....first go to Go Daddy (see ONLINE RESOURCES at the end of this section) and purchase a website address, then use Elance to post your project for freelance web designers from all around the world to bid on your project. For less than $500 (I've had them done for $150 before) you can have a first class website built. All you really need is a basic 1-3 page website. If you really don't want to spend much money then just have a one page website designed with your bar's name, contact information, location, pictures of your place, and menu. Whenever you post your website design project on Elance also include that you would like to have the ability to change portions of the text from time to time on your own. This will help you add info about upcoming promotions and parties.

Pro Tip: Forget about having fancy flashing pictures or other complicated bells and whistles added into your design. Not only are they expensive, but they block your website's content from search engines, so they wind up hurting search results anyway.

2) Promotional Email

There are companies out there that make it extremely easy to manage e-mail marketing campaigns. Companies such as AWeber Communications help create appealing newsletters and promotional e-mails and then send them out on the dates of your choice. Believe me it's a lot more efficient and professional then sending out your own plain text e-mails once a week. The companies that provide these services also know how to keep e-mails from being filtered into junk folders. If you send e-mails on your own, chances are you won't reach as many people's inboxes as you think.

3) Social Media

Online social media sources are a great way to market your bar and most importantly they are free advertising. Start a Facebook, MySpace, and Twitter account and make friends with other groups in the area and invite them into your bar. Social media sites are another great place to update your customers on parties and promotions that are happening at your bar.

4) Search Engines

Always register your businesses with the 2 largest search engines, Google and Yahoo right away. When people do an internet search for bars in your area, you'll want to make sure that your physical address and telephone number show up. Once you have a website address you can also register that as well.
Mobile Marketing Campaign

Text Message Promotions

Everyone texts these days. Even my mom texts, which is completely scary when I come to think about it. People have become so glued to their cell phones that it would be a shame to not take advantage of text promotions. Mobile promotions are relatively cheap and boy do they get the word out fast. There are many companies out there that specialize in mobile marketing and I've included a few in the ONLINE RESOURCES of this section, so check them out.

The mobile marketing companies can help you set up giveaway promotions at your bar where customers text a code to enter. This will not only create entertainment for your customers, but it will allow you to grow your database of numbers every time a customer texts in to participate.

Local Marketing Campaign

1) Local Media

Local newspapers, magazines, radio, and/or television advertisements are good avenues to explore if the publication or channel is popular in the area. Personally I never like to spend a lot of money here because I know that if I spend time networking, I can get just as good results for a lot less money. If you do want to purchase an advertisement in your local area, make sure you always negotiate the advertising costs. Never go with the first number they quote you.

2) Networking

Person to person contact is so neglected with all of the available technology these days. I make it a point of taking one night out of the week to visit other bars and invite staff members and people I meet over to my bar. Bar employees love to drink and can be fantastic customers. I sometimes offer to buy them a drink if they stop by my place, because I know that once they come through the door they never stay for just one drink.

Pro Tip: I also make a point of attending local community events as well as sponsoring local adult sports teams. It may cost a few hundred dollars to sponsor an adult baseball or soccer team, but the profits you will make in return are well worth it. Every team I've ever sponsored comes in after their games and drinks a ton. Sometimes they even bring the opposing team as well. Game nights always bring in good profits and the initial investment is so minimal when you look at the big picture.

3) Phone Book Listing

The phone book isn't really going to bring you many new customers, but you can annoy a lot of people if you aren't listed. Make sure you have a basic listing that includes your phone and address and don't waste your money on an ad, it's not worth it!

ONLINE RESOURCES:

1) http://www.elance.com
Great place to hire a freelance web designer to create an attractive website for your bar.

2) http://www.godaddy.com
Use Go Daddy to purchase a domain name and website hosting for your bar.
3) http://maps.google.com
Use this site to register your bar with Google. Click on "Put your business on Google maps" to get started. You will first have to create a login before you can add your listing.

4) http://listings.local.yahoo.com/csubmit/index.php
Register your bar with yahoo through this link.

5) http://www.aweber.com
AWeber offers extensive e-mail marketing campaigns with high delivery rates, easy to use templates for creating e-mails, as well as ways to track your progress. The best part is that you can set your e-mail campaign on automatic and AWeber will send the e-mails out on the dates you choose ahead of time.

6) http://www.clubtexting.com
Club Texting offers mobile messaging packages that allow you to pay as you go.

7) http://www.textmeforbusiness.com
This mobile messaging company offers larger text messaging packages.

8) http://www.facebook.com , http://www.myspace.com , http://twitter.com
These are a few of the most popular social media networking websites to utilize in your marketing campaign.

Phase 5: Open to the Public Summary
Attack Steps Simultaneously

Step 24: Plan an Opening Strategy
- Progressing through a few stages of opening (i.e. friends and family party, soft opening, invitation only party) gives you a chance to improve operations and product issues before the grand opening party.

Step 25: Begin Marketing Plan
- A proper marketing campaign for your bar should include internet marketing, mobile marketing, and local marketing.
- Internet marketing includes building a website, promotional e-mails, social media, and registering with search engines.
- Mobile marketing is very effective for letting customers know about promotional parties and events.
- Don't underestimate the power of face to face networking in your community.....it's memorable, underused, and costs less than other forms of marketing.

Conclusion

Congratulations, you now have the knowledge you need to open your bar. What you decide to do with this knowledge is entirely up to you! You can continue to make excuses for why you can't start a bar or you can take control of your life and financial future and get started today. If you don't have enough money, set up a weekly savings plan. If your credit is bad, start a plan to improve it. I went into this business from being a bouncer for a biker bar, $20k in debt, and having an awful credit score to almost 10 years later, selling 5 bars, paying off my debt, buying a house, and having enough savings to take 2 years off to travel and create this program.

Taking risks in life isn't comfortable, but living day to day barely getting by isn't exactly comfortable either. I challenge you to take a few more risks in your life. Sometimes, even when things don't go as planned, you learn valuable lessons that lead to other successes. I view life as a game and I always play to win. How you live your life is your choice.

Down the road when you start your bar, remember to use my website, Barin30Daysorless.com as a resource. On the "Bar Tips" page I continually add useful links to online companies and services that bar owners can utilize to help save time and money. I also offer a membership program called "The Fast Track" for bar owners that gives access to important PDF files for operating procedures, cost control, employee rules and regulations, as well as access to informational videos. I plan on launching more products to help you in the future, so stay tuned.

Thank you for your support and I wish you the best of luck. I look forward to having a drink with you in your bar one day in the near future.

Best Wishes,

Todd R. McGlamery

Additional Resources

Hiring Document: Bartender (example)

I, _____, have received and read a copy of the Employee Handbook which outlines the policies and expectations required of me at _____(bar's name).

I understand that as **Bartender** my possible responsibilities include, but are not limited to:

1. Follow opening & closing procedures.
2. Know all bar pricing.
3. Keep track of bar inventory and count cash register.
4. Stock bar with necessary products (i.e. beer, wine, liquor, condiments, glasses, napkins, ice, etc.), maintain all equipment and tools, and control and limit waste.
5. Attend all staff meetings.
6. Follow bar regulations and instructions set by management.
7. Follow health and safety regulations.
8. Interact positively with customers and stay attentive.
9. Manage customer alcohol consumption and check IDs.
10. Communicate problems to management and communicate appropriately with coworkers during shift.

I have familiarized myself with the contents of the handbook and list of responsibilities set before me. By my signature below, I acknowledge, understand, accept and agree to comply with the information contained in the Employee Handbook provided to me as well as my responsibilities. I understand this handbook is not intended to cover every situation, which may arise during my employment, but is simply a general guide to the policies and expectations of _____(bar's name).

I further understand that I will be paid an hourly wage of $3 per hour (plus tips) on a semi-monthly basis.

_____   _____
Signature   Date

Hiring Document: Cook (example)

I, _____, have received and read a copy of the Employee Handbook which outlines the policies and expectations required of me at _____(bar's name).

I understand that as a **Cook** my possible responsibilities include, but are not limited to:

1. Follow opening & closing procedures.
2. Prep all food for the day in an orderly and timely manner and re-stock menu items when needed.
3. Manage food inventory, place orders when needed, and control and limit waste.
4. Follow bar regulations and instructions set by management.
5. Follow health and safety regulations.
6. Maintain high product quality and product consistency.
7. Communicate specials for the day and any shortages to staff members.
8. Always keep the kitchen area clean and maintain all equipment and tools.
9. Attend all staff meetings.
10. Communicate problems to the manager and communicate with servers regarding customer satisfaction of meals.

I have familiarized myself with the contents of the handbook and list of responsibilities set before me. By my signature below, I acknowledge, understand, accept and agree to comply with the information contained in the Employee Handbook provided to me as well as my responsibilities. I understand this handbook is not intended to cover every situation, which may arise during my employment, but is simply a general guide to the policies and expectations of _____(bar's name).

I further understand that I will be paid an hourly wage of $10 per hour on a semi-monthly basis.

_____   _____
Signature   Date

Hiring Document: Server (example)

I, _____, have received and read a copy of the Employee Handbook which outlines the policies and expectations required of me at _____(bar's name).

I understand that as a **Server** my possible responsibilities include, but are not limited to:

1. Follow opening and closing procedures.
2. Maintain a neat and clean appearance.
3. Greet customers with a smile and serve them quickly. Stay attentive during their visit and thank them for coming in.
4. Know all bar pricing of menu items and daily specials.
5. Up-sell when appropriate.
6. Follow bar regulations and instructions set by management.
7. Follow health and safety regulations.
8. Attend all staff meetings.
9. Communicate problems to the manager and communicate appropriately with coworkers during shifts.
10. Keep tables and chairs neat and clean and help bartender in any way possible.

I have familiarized myself with the contents of the handbook and list of responsibilities set before me. By my signature below, I acknowledge, understand, accept and agree to comply with the information contained in the Employee Handbook provided to me as well as my responsibilities. I understand this handbook is not intended to cover every situation, which may arise during my employment, but is simply a general guide to the policies and expectations of _____(bar's name).

I further understand that I will be paid an hourly wage of $2.13 per hour (plus tips) on a semi-monthly basis.

_____   _____
Signature   Date

Hiring Document: Manager (example)

I, _____, have received and read a copy of the Employee Handbook which outlines the policies and expectations required of me at _____(bar's name).

I understand that as a **Manager** my possible responsibilities include, but are not limited to:

1. Follow opening and closing procedures.
2. Check inventory records in bar and kitchen as well as inventory orders placed.
3. Oversee marketing efforts, entertainment, and parties to increase business.
4. Communicate positively with staff members and stay on top of training and performance.
5. Arrange weekly staff meetings and create weekly staff schedule.
6. Solve any problems that arise with customers.
7. Check product quality and consistency.
8. Follow bar regulations and instructions set by management.
9. Follow health and safety regulations.
10. Communicate with customers to obtain feedback on products and service.

I have familiarized myself with the contents of the handbook and list of responsibilities set before me. By my signature below, I acknowledge, understand, accept and agree to comply with the information contained in the Employee Handbook provided to me as well as my responsibilities. I understand this handbook is not intended to cover every situation, which may arise during my employment, but is simply a general guide to the policies and expectations of _____(bar's name).

I further understand that I will be paid based on a weekly salary of $600 on a semi-monthly basis.

_____   _____
Signature   Date

State Agencies Responsible for Alcohol Licenses, Laws, and/or Control

Alabama
Alcoholic Beverage Control Board
Phone: (334) 271-3840
http://www.abc.alabama.gov/index.aspx

Alaska
Revenue Department Alcoholic Beverage Control Board
5848 E. Tudor Road,   Anchorage, AK 99507
Phone: (907) 269-0350
http://www.dps.alaska.gov/abc/

Arizona
Department of Liquor Licenses and Control
800 W. Washington, 5th Floor,   Phoenix, AZ 85007
Phone: (602) 542-5141
http://www.azliquor.gov/

Arkansas
Alcohol Beverage Control
Phone: (501) 682-1105
http://www.dfa.arkansas.gov/offices/abc/

California
Department of Alcoholic Beverage Control
3927 Lennane Drive, Suite 100,   Sacramento, CA 95834
Phone: (916) 419-2500
http://www.abc.ca.gov/

Board of Equalization
P.O. Box 942879,   Sacramento, CA 94279
Phone: (800) 400-7115
www.boe.ca.gov

Colorado
Department of Revenue-Liquor Enforcement Division
Denver: 1881 Pierce #108A,   Lakewood, CO 80214-1495
Phone: (303) 205-2300
Colorado Springs: 4420 Austin Bluffs Pkwy, Colorado Springs, CO 80918
Phone: (719) 594-8702
Greeley: 2320 Reservoir Road, Ste A, Greeley, CO 80634
Phone: (970) 356-3992

Grand Junction: 222 S. 6th St. Ste 425, Grand Junction, CO 81501
Phone: (970) 248-7133
http://www.colorado.gov/revenue/liquor

Connecticut
Department of Consumer Protection
165 Capitol Ave,   Hartford, CT 06106
Phone: (860) 713-6050
http://www.ct.gov/dcp/site/default.asp

Delaware
Department of Public Services   Alcoholic Beverage Control Commission
Carvel State Office Building, 820 N. French Street, 3rd Floor,   Wilmington, DE 19801
Phone: (302) 577-52222
http://date.delaware.gov/dabcpublic/index.jsp

District of Columbia
Alcoholic Beverage Regulation Administration
1250 U Street, NW, Third Floor,   Washington, DC 20009
Phone: (202) 442-4423
http://abra.dc.gov/DC/ABRA/

Florida
Division of Alcoholic Beverages and Tobacco
1940 North Monroe Street,   Tallahassee, Florida 32399
Phone: (850) 487-1395
http://www.myfloridalicense.com/dbpr/abt/index.html

Georgia
Department of Revenue   Alcohol & Tobacco Tax Division
1800 Century Blvd., N.E. Room 4235,   Atlanta, Georgia 30345
Phone: (404) 417-4900
https://etax.dor.ga.gov/BusTax_Alcohol.aspx

Hawaii
Honolulu: Liquor Commission
Pacific Park Plaza,   711 Kapiolani Blvd, Suite 600   Honolulu, Hawaii 96813
Phone: (808) 768-7300
http://www.co.honolulu.hi.us/liq/
Hawaii
Office of Liquor Control
101 Aupuni Street, Suite 230   Hilo, Hawaii 96720

Phone: East Hi: (808) 961-8218   West Hi: (808) 327-3549
http://www.hawaii-county.com/directory/dir_liquor.htm

Kauai
Department of Liquor Control
Lihu'e Civic Center   Mo'ikeha Building,   4444 Rice Street, Suite 120,   Lihu'e, Kauai, Hawaii 96766
Phone: (808) 241-4966
http://www.kauai.gov/Government/Departments/LiquorControl/tabid/128/Default.aspx

Maui
Department of Liquor Control
2145 Kaohu Street, Room 105,   Wailuku, HI 96793
Phone: (808) 243-7753
788 Pauoa Stree, Room 102, Lahaina, HI 96761
Phone: (808) 661-9581
http://www.mauicounty.gov/index.aspx?nid=667

Idaho
Liquor Division Administrative Office
1349 East Beechcraft Court   Boise, ID 83716
Phone: (208) 947-9400
Alcohol Beverage Control
P.O. Box 700, Meridian, ID 83680
Phone: (208) 884-7060
http://www.liquor.idaho.gov/

Illinois
Liquor Control Commission
Chicago:
100 West Randolph Street,   Suite 7-801,   Chicago, IL 60601
Phone: (312) 814-2206
Springfield:
101 West Jefferson Suite 3-525   Springfield, Illinois 62702
Phone: (217) 782-2136
http://www.state.il.us/lcc/

Indiana
Alcohol and Tobacco Commission
Indiana Government Center South, Room E-114,   302 W. Washington Street, Indianapolis, IN 46204
Phone: (317) 232-2430
http://www.in.gov/atc/

Iowa
Alcoholic Beverages Division
1918 S.E. Hulsizer Avenue,   Ankeny, IA 50021
Phone: (866) 469-2223
http://iowaabd.com/

Kansas
Department of Revenue Alcoholic Beverage Control
915 SW Harrison Street, Room 214,   Topeka, KS 66625-3512
Phone: (785) 296-7015
http://www.ksrevenue.org/abc.htm

Kentucky
Alcoholic Beverage Control Department
1003 Twilight Trail,   Frankfort, Kentucky 40601
Phone: (502) 564-4850
http://abc.ky.gov/

Louisiana
Department of Revenue   Alcohol and Tobacco Control Office
8585 Archives Avenue, Suite 220   Baton Rouge, Louisiana 70809
Phone: (225) 925-4041
http://www.atc.rev.state.la.us/

Maine
Liquor Licensing & Compliance Division
45 Commerce Drive, Suite 1,   Augusta, Maine 04333
Phone: (207) 624-7220
http://www.maine.gov/dps/liqr/

Maryland
Comptroller of Maryland
Revenue Administration Division
Motor-fuel, Alcohol and Tobacco Tax Unit
P.O. Box 2999,   Annapolis, MD 21404
Phone: (410) 260-7131
http://www.comp.state.md.us/

Montgomery County Dept. Of Liquor Control
16650 Crabs Branch Way, Rockville, MD 20855
Phone: (240) 777-1900
http://www.montgomerycountymd.gov/dlctmpl.asp?url=/content/dlc/liquor/home/index.asp

Massachusetts
Alcoholic Beverages Control Commission
239 Causeway Street,   Boston, MA 02114
Phone: (617) 727-3040
http://www.mass.gov/abcc/

Michigan
Liquor Control Commission
P.O. Box 30005   Lansing, MI 48909
Phone: (517) 322-1345
http://www.michigan.gov/dleg/

Minnesota
Department of Public Safety
Alcohol and Gambling and Enforcement Division
444 Cedar St., Suite 222,   St. Paul, Minnesota 55101
Phone: (651) 201-7500
http://www.dps.state.mn.us/alcgamb/alcgamb.aspx

Mississippi
Alcoholic Beverage Control Office
P.O. Box 1033,   Jackson, Mississippi 39215
Phone: (601) 923-7000
http://www.dor.ms.gov/

Missouri
Department of Public Safety   Liquor Control Division
1738 E. Elm, Lower Level, Jefferson City, Missouri 65101
Phone: (573) 751-2333
http://www.atc.dps.mo.gov/index.asp

Montana
Liquor License Bureau
P.O. Box 1712   Helena, Montana 59604
Phone: (866) 859-2254
http://revenue.mt.gov/default.mcpx

Nebraska
Liquor Control Commission
301 Centennial Mall South,   P.O. Box 95046   Lincoln, Nebraska 68509-5046
Phone: (402) 471-2571
http://www.lcc.ne.gov/

Nevada
Department of Taxation
http://tax.state.nv.us/
Carson City: 1550 College Parkway Suite 115,   Carson City, NV 89706
Phone: (775) 684-2000
Reno:
Phone: (775) 687-9999
Henderson/Las Vegas:
Phone: (702) 486-2300
New Hampshire
Liquor Commission
50 Storrs Street,   Concord, New Hampshire 03301
Phone: (603) 271-7549
http://webster.state.nh.us/liquor/

New Jersey
Department of Law and Public Safety   Division of Alcoholic Beverage Control
140 East Front Street,   Trenton, New Jersey 08625
Phone: (609) 984-2830
http://www.state.nj.us/lps/abc/index.html

New Mexico
Regulation & Licensing Department
Alcohol and Gaming Division
2550 Cerrillos Road, Santa Fe, New Mexico 87505
Phone: (505) 476-4875
www.rld.state.nm.us/agd/

Department of Public Safety
Special Investigations Division
6301 Indian School NE, Suite 310,   Albuquerque NM 87110
Phone: (505) 841-8053
http://www.dps.nm.org/lawEnforcement/sid/index.php

New York
State Liquor Authority
80 S. Swan Street, 9th floor, Albany, NY 12210
Phone: (518) 474-3114
http://www.abc.state.ny.us/

North Carolina
Alcoholic Beverage Control Commission
3322 Garner Road,   Raleigh, North Carolina 27610

Phone: (919) 779-0700
http://www.ncabc.com/

North Dakota
Office of the State Tax Commissioner
Alcohol Tax Section
600 East Boulevard Avenue, Bismarck, North Dakota 58505-0599
Phone: (701) 328-7088
http://www.nd.gov/tax/alcohol/

Ohio
Department of Commerce   Division Of Liquor Control
6606 Tussing Road,   Reynoldsburg, Ohio 43068
Phone: (614) 644-2360
http://com.ohio.gov/liqr/

Oklahoma
Alcoholic Beverage Laws Enforcement Commission
4545 N. Lincoln Blvd.   Suite #270,   Oklahoma City, Oklahoma 73105
Phone: (405) 521-3484
http://www.able.state.ok.us/

Oregon
Liquor Control Commission
9079 SE McLoughlin Blvd.,   Portland, Oregon 97222
Phone: (503) 872-5000
http://www.oregon.gov/OLCC/index.shtml

Pennsylvania
Liquor Control Board
Northwest Office Building,   Harrisburg, PA 17124-0001
Phone: (717) 783-7637
http://www.lcb.state.pa.us/

Rhode Island
Department of Business Regulation   Liquor Control Administration
1511 Pontiac Avenue, Cranston, RI 02920
Phone: (401) 462-9500
http://www.dbr.state.ri.us/divisions/commlicensing/liquor.php

South Carolina
Department of Revenue & Taxation: Alcohol Beverage Licensing 301 Gervais St.,   P.O.

Box 125, Columbia, South Carolina 29212-0907
Phone: (803) 898-5864
http://www.sctax.org/Tax+Information/abl/default.htm

South Dakota
Department of Revenue Division of Special Taxes & Licensing
445 East Capitol Avenue, Pierre, South Dakota 57501-2276
Phone: (605) 773-3311
http://www.state.sd.us/drr2/propspectax/index.htm

Tennessee
Alcoholic Beverage Commission
226 Capitol Blvd. Building, Suite 300, Nashville, TN 37243-0755
Phone: (615) 741-1602
http://www.state.tn.us/abc

Texas
Alcoholic Beverage Commission
5806 Mesa Drive, P.O. Box 13127, Austin, Texas 78731
Phone: (512) 206-3333
http://www.tabc.state.tx.us/

Utah
Department of Alcoholic Beverage Control
1625 S. 900 West, Salt Lake City, Utah 84104
Phone: (801) 977-6800
http://www.alcbev.state.ut.us/

Vermont
Department of Liquor Control
13 Green Mountain Drive, Montpelier, Vermont 05620-4501
Phone: (802) 828-2345
http://www.state.vt.us/dlc/

Virginia
Department of Alcoholic Beverage Control
2901 Hermitage Road, Richmond, VA 23220
Phone: (804) 213-4400
http://www.abc.state.va.us/

Washington
Liquor Control Board
3000 Pacific Avenue SE, Olympia, Washington 98504-3075
Phone: (360) 664-1600
www.liq.wa.gov/

West Virginia
Alcohol Beverage Control Administration
322 70th St. S.E.,   Charleston, West Virginia 25304
Phone: (304) 558-2481
www.abca.wv.gov/

Wisconsin
Alcohol & Tobacco Enforcement   Department of Revenue
2135 Rimrock Road, Madison, Wisconsin 53713
Phone: (608) 266-2772
http://www.dor.state.wi.us/

Wyoming
Liquor Association
P.O. Box 1894
Cheyenne, Wyoming 82003
(307) 634-6484
http://wyoliquor.org/

Department of Revenue: Liquor Division
Phone: (307) 777-6448
http://eliquor.wyoming.gov/

Puerto Rico
Office of the Comptroller, Commonwealth of Puerto Rico, P.O. Box 366 069 San Juan,
PR 00936-6069
Phone: (787) 754-3030
http://www.ocpr.gov.pr/

Canada
Liquor Control and Licensing Branch (LCLB)
Phone: (604) 660-2421
www.hsd.gov.bc.ca/lclb/

Made in the USA
San Bernardino, CA
15 July 2014